ARCADIA PUBLIC LIBRARY
ARCADIA, WISCONSIN 54612

P9-CME-595

The
Flannel Board
Storytelling
Book

The Flannel Board Storytelling Book

BY JUDY SIERRA

THE H. W. WILSON COMPANY

1987

027.62
Sie

Copyright © 1987 by Judy Sierra.

All rights reserved. No part of this work may be reproduced or copied in any form or by any means, including but not restricted to graphic, electronic, and mechanical—for example, photocopying, recording, taping, or information retrieval systems—without the express written permission of the publisher, except that a reviewer may quote and a magazine or newspaper may print brief passages in a review written specifically for inclusion in that magazine or newspaper.

"The Fish with the Deep Sea Smile" from *Nibble, Nibble* by Margaret Wise Brown. Copyright © 1938 by E. P. Dutton, copyright renewal © 1965 by Roberta B. Rauch. Reprinted by permission.

First Printing 1987
Second Printing 1988

Library of Congress Cataloging-in-Publication Data

Sierra, Judy.
    The flannel board storytelling book.

    Bibliography:
✔ 1. Storytelling. 2. Flannelgraphs. 3. Libraries,
Children's—Activity programs. 4. Teaching—Aids and
devices. I. Title.
Z718.3.S55 1987   027.62′51   87–6260
ISBN 0-8242-0747-5

Printed in the United States of America

Acknowledgments

Thanks to Bob Kaminski for advice, support, proofreading and dinners; to Joan Gardner of the Los Angeles Public Library for her thoughtful reading of the manuscript; and especially to the children of California and New Mexico who have listened to my stories and acted them out with puppets and panache.

Table of Contents

Introduction

Flannel board storytelling is a wonderful way to share stories, poems, and songs visually with children while keeping the intimacy and spontaneity of traditional storytelling. It is an art that is widely practiced by teachers and librarians. These storytellers may not realize that they are part of an ancient and worldwide tradition.[†] Countless generations of storytellers have used figures and drawings both to entertain their listeners and to help themselves remember their tales. The use of a cloth board and felt figures, though, appears to be a recent innovation. But unlike other modern media, flannel boards are as warm and personal as storytelling itself.

A flannel board is simply a rectangle of wood or sturdy cardboard that has been covered with flannel or a similar fabric. The flannel board is set upright on a stand or table, and figures cut from nonwoven fabric are placed on it, enabling the storyteller to illustrate a story as it is told. The flannel board and figures can be easily and inexpensively made: with a small investment of time and money, you can present stories that are a truly special, eagerly anticipated event for your group.

Flannel board stories are told without a book. This allows you to make more direct contact with your listeners. If you have been wanting to tell stories but didn't know exactly how to begin, flannel board storytelling is the ideal way to move from story-reading into traditional storytelling.

[†] *See* Anne Pellowski, *The World of Storytelling* (R. R. Bowker, 1977), pp. 135–150.

This book contains thirty-six stories, songs, and poems from many countries, reflecting rich and diverse cultures. Some are old favorites, some you may not yet be familiar with. I have adapted and retold most of them for use with the flannel board. Suggestions for participatory activities follow each story. These include oral participation during the flannel board story, as well as dramatizing the story for puppetry and creative dramatics. In these ways, storytelling extends from being a listening experience into a language development activity.

The stories have been divided into two groups: those especially for three- to five-year-olds, and those for five- to eight-year-olds. This division is a general one, and you may find that your group enjoys stories designated for older or younger children.

Beyond this book, you will find other stories that adapt well to the flannel board, and you may even make up your own. Simple stories with strong plots, repetitive stories, and cumulative stories usually work particularly well. A picture book that is too small to share with a large group can be adapted for flannel board telling. Once you have told some of the stories in this book, you will develop a feel for the elements that make for a good flannel board story.

Enjoy!

The Flannel Board

Flannel boards are available commercially through school supply companies. They usually come with an adjustable tripod stand, and, if your budget allows, are a good investment.

It is fairly simple and inexpensive to make a flannel board for yourself. A rectangle of cardboard or wood is covered with one of the fabrics described below. The story figures in this book are designed to be used on a board that is 20″ wide by 16″ high. If your board is larger than this, you will probably want to enlarge the patterns for figures on an enlarging photocopier.

A flannel board that folds to protect the cloth surface can be made from an artist's portfolio (available at art supply stores). Choose one that has ribbon ties on three sides: when you are using it to tell stories, open it up and tie the two sets of side ribbons with about five inches of slack, making it into a self-supporting triangular unit which will sit up nicely on a table or chair.

Its name notwithstanding, a flannel board does not need to be covered with flannel; many other fabrics are more durable and come in better colors. Any fabric that has a fuzzy nap or pile will work, with the exception of stretch fabrics, which will sag. My favorite is a fabric called acrylic fleece. The story figures adhere to the board through a combination of friction and static electricity between the fibers.

Cut the cloth so that it will overlap the board by the thickness of the board plus two inches. Clip diagonally across the corners of the cloth to eliminate bunching. Glue the fabric to the back of the board with a strong white glue (such as Sobo or Tacky), and tape or thumbtack the cloth to hold it in place while the glue dries.

When using a portfolio, you will only be covering one-half of the inside surface, so the cloth will overlap on only three sides. The fourth edge of the cloth will just meet the center inside fold of the portfolio, where you can glue down the edge.

To cover a piece of plywood, use a staple gun or tacks to attach the cloth to the back of the board.

Flannel boards are traditionally blue, brown, or black. A neutral blue is a good choice, since few flannel board characters are blue in color—a figure the same color as the background would be difficult for the children to see.

Your board should be kept covered when not in use, as dirt will make it lose its cling. You may also need to charge up its static electricity and pick up its fibers occasionally by brushing it with a soft plastic nail brush or hair brush. One great advantage of the homemade flannel board is that you can easily re-cover it when the cloth wears out.

Making Story Figures for the Flannel Board

Story figures have traditionally been made from felt. Medium or heavy weight nonwoven, nonfusible interfacing (available at fabric stores—the salespeople will know what you are talking about!) is easier to use than felt. You can see through it to trace patterns right from the book, and it accepts markers, watercolor paints, and crayon almost as well as paper. Felt is more opaque and also difficult to color. Interfacing is recommended for almost all small and medium-sized figures in this book, with felt as a second choice. Paper figures, backed with felt or sandpaper, are *not* recommended, as many of the figures in this book need to overlap and cling to each other.

Felt is preferable for most larger pieces, such as trees and other scenery, and also for items such as chairs and tables that need to be a solid color. The extra surface fibers of felt make large pieces adhere more securely to the flannel board, and the use of colored felt eliminates the need to color large areas. The instructions following each story suggest which pieces to cut from felt.

When buying felt, purchase the precut squares, not the felt that is sold by the yard. The squares have been treated to stay crisp and stiff, but the felt off the bolt becomes wrinkled, and figures lose their shape.

If you need to color the felt, use medium or broad tipped markers and make short, heavy strokes or dots. Detail can be added by gluing on pieces of contrasting felt, yarn, sequins, etc. Take care, though, not to add too much weight, or the piece will roll off the flannel board!

Nonwoven interfacing can be colored with markers, watercolors, or heavily pigmented crayons (available at art supply stores). When using markers, it is easy to get carried away and saturate the figure with dark colors, but this makes them uninteresting and difficult to see from a distance. It is better to color the figures with bright or pastel shades, and then use a dark color for outlines and defining lines.

Vary the texture of your figures by using a series of short strokes in several colors for fur, using cross-hatching to simulate wood or fabric and curlicues for feathers. Give figures a three-dimensional look by bringing strokes of color in from the edges of each color area, using heavy pressure at the edge and tapering up and off toward the middle. It is easier to color the figures before cutting them out. Since markers, watercolors, and crayons will eventually smudge, you may wish to give heavily used figures a spray of fixative for water colors (available at art supply stores).

Many of the stories in this book take place inside and outside houses. Here is a method of making the outline of a house easily using yarn and straight pins:

Place five straight pins into the flannel board, one for each of the four corners of the house (side view) and one for the peak of the roof. Place the pins almost parallel to the board, with the head and about ¼" sticking out, the rest of the pin between the cloth and the board, the tip of the pin sticking into the board underneath. Angle all five pins toward the center of the house. Wrap a piece of bright-colored yarn around the five pins to outline the house shape. If children will be using the flannel board, and the pins would be a hazard to them, cut ½" wide strips of felt and use them to form the house outline.

The following is a basic list of supplies to get started making figures for flannel board stories:

One-half yard of white, nonwoven, nonfusible interfacing;
6 to 8 felt squares in green, brown, tan, grey, blue, and white;
Set of medium-tipped markers (the more colors the better); permanent markers are best, since colors won't smudge;
Small bottle of fabric glue, such as Sobo or Tacky;
Good, sharp scissors.

Telling Stories with the Flannel Board

Specific directions follow each story, but here are some general guidelines for successful use of the flannel board:

Stories should be learned and told, not read. This is an opportunity for you to establish the direct rapport of storytelling, using the figures to aid your memory and add visual interest for the audience. Poems, songs, and some stories, such as "This Is the House That Jack Built" and "Master of All Masters," need to be learned and told word for word. The other stories can be learned verbatim, or, if you are like many storytellers, you will learn the basic plot and dialogue, and some of the more important and colorful phrases, but tell the story mostly in your own words. The stories in this book are given in simple and straightforward versions, without much description. Feel free to embroider them to satisfy yourself and your listeners.

It's not a good idea, though, to simplify or explain the stories. Storytelling is the recounting of the events of once-upon-a-time as if you had been there, and you had heard and seen everything. Interpretation is up to the listener.

Practice telling the stories to a friend, or into a tape recorder, without the book. Then rehearse telling the story with the flannel board and figures at least three times. You will find it is essential to decide in advance where and when to place each figure, so that the storytelling and placing of story figures flow naturally. Sit to one side of the board and hold the figures, in order, face up on your lap.

Move the figures as little as possible, in keeping with the sense of the story, during the storytelling: they are illustrations of the story events, not puppets. The children's imaginations will fill in the details that you describe. You should be able to spend most of your time telling the story to the children and watching their reactions, reaching over occasionally to add, move, remove, or point to the story figures. As a general rule, it is best not to move the figures while you are talking, but to pause while you place or move a figure on the flannel board.

Extending the Stories through Participation

Some stories stand on their own as literary listening experiences. Others beg for the audience to join in and participate in the storytelling, and/or to act the story out with puppets or through creative dramatics. For those in this splendid second category, some simple guidelines are included concerning participation and follow-up activities. A good story can be appreciated many times and in many ways.

In some cases, I have recommended that you use the flannel board patterns to trace, cut, and color cardboard stick puppets (use pencils, chopsticks, or dowels as rods). The story can then be acted out by the puppets behind the flannel board—using the top edge as a stage—or in a simple cardboard box puppet stage. Creative dramatics is suggested as a follow-up activity for other stories. Books on storytelling, puppetry, and creative dramatics are included in the bibliography.

Some other ways to extend children's use of the flannel board are: encouraging them to use the figures to tell the stories themselves; having them make their own figures to tell either original tales or stories and poems from books; and letting them use flannel board figures to present book reports or reports in various subject areas.

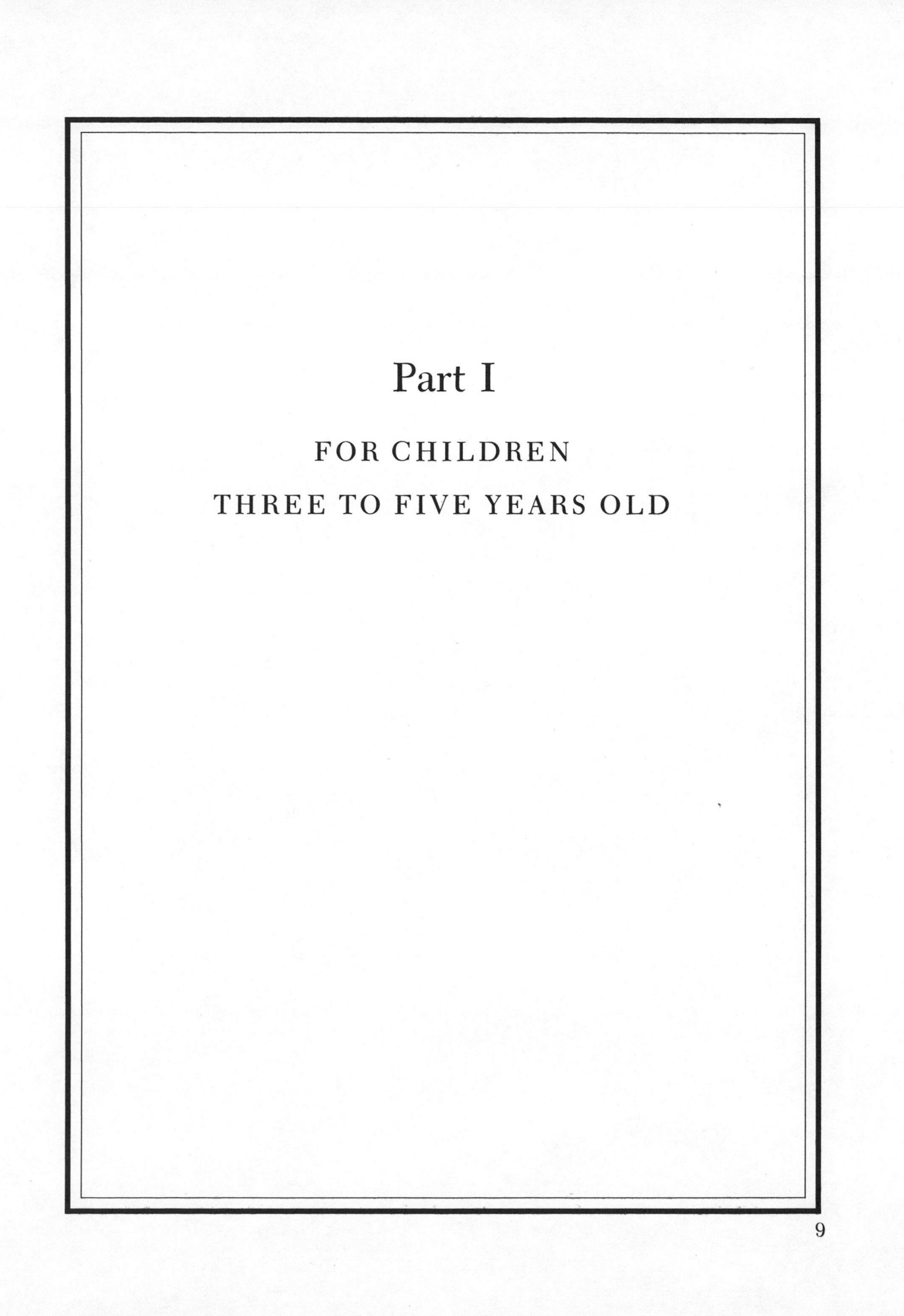

Part I

FOR CHILDREN
THREE TO FIVE YEARS OLD

Five Little Chickens

A TRADITIONAL ENGLISH RHYME

Said the first little chicken,
With a queer little squirm,
"I wish I could find
A fat little worm."

Said the second little chicken,
With an odd little shrug,
"I wish I could find
A fat little bug."

Said the third little chicken,
With a sharp little squeal,
"I wish I could find
Some nice yellow meal."

Said the fourth little chicken,
With a sigh of grief,
"I wish I could find
A little green leaf."

Said the fifth little chicken,
With a faint little moan,
"I wish I could find
A wee gravel stone."

"Now see here," said the mother,
From the green garden patch,
"If you want any breakfast,
Just come here and SCRATCH!"

DIRECTIONS

Mother hen sits on the right side of the flannel board, on top of a mound of dirt cut from brown felt and pinned to the flannel board with straight pins or safety pins (hidden under the felt). Cut five slits in the felt, as shown by the dotted lines on the pattern, and slide the five little chickens' treasures into them, so the children can just barely see them, but with enough sticking out that you can grasp to pull them out.

Cut the five little chickens from the same pattern, then color them differently. Place them on the left side of the flannel board, one by one, as you recite the poem.

Participation

The fun continues after the poem is over: ask the group, "Now, what did that first little chicken want?" Then place the first little chicken near the mother, pull out the worm, and place it on the little chicken's beak, and so on for all five.

As the children learn the words of the poem, you may narrate and have either individual children, or the whole group, say the words of the five little chickens and the mother hen.

The House in the Woods

A NORWEGIAN TALE

A SHEEP was tired of living in the sheepfold, and he decided to go out and build himself a house in the woods. On his way out of the barnyard, he met a pig.

"Where are you going?" asked the pig.

"I am tired of living in the sheepfold," answered the sheep. "I am going to build myself a house in the woods."

"May I come with you?" asked the pig. "I am tired of living in the pigpen."

"Perhaps," said the sheep. "What can you do to help?"

"I can roll the logs for the house with my snout," answered the pig.

"Come along, then," said the sheep. "I can surely use a helper like you!"

The sheep and the pig walked along together, and they met a goose.

"Where are you going?" asked the goose.

"We are tired of living in the sheepfold and the pigpen," answered the pig. "We are going to build ourselves a house in the woods."

"May I come with you?" begged the goose. "I am tired of living in the poultryyard."

"Perhaps," said the pig. "What can you do to help?"

"I can gather moss with my beak, and stuff it into the chinks between the logs," answered the goose.

14

"Come along, then," said the pig. "We can surely use a helper like you!"

The sheep and the pig and the goose walked along together, and they met a rooster.

"Where are you going?" asked the rooster.

"We are tired of living in the sheepfold and the pigpen and the poultryyard," said the goose. "We are going to build ourselves a house in the woods."

"May I come with you?" asked the rooster.

"Perhaps," said the goose. "What can you do to help?"

"I can crow 'cock-a-doodle-doo' and wake you up every morning," answered the rooster.

"Come along, then," said the goose. "We can surely use a helper like you!"

The sheep and the pig and the goose and the rooster walked out of the barnyard, and they walked, and they walked, and they walked, until they reached a clearing in the woods. Then, the sheep ate all the grass in the clearing, the pig rolled up some big logs with his snout, and they made a house. The goose gathered moss with his beak and stuffed it into the cracks between the logs.

The four animals lived happily together in the house in the woods, and every morning, the rooster crowed "cock-a-doodle-doo" and woke them all up.

Follow-up

After you have told this story several times, choose four children to act it out in creative dramatics. The four children will say the words of the sheep, pig, goose, and rooster, and at the end of the story, they will mime the building of an imaginary three-dimensional house. You can involve all the children either by having several groups act out the story in succession, with the rest watching, or by having the groups act it out simultaneously, in different parts of the room, as you narrate.

DIRECTIONS

Color the four animals on both sides. Each animal will face the sheep when they first meet, then turn around (flip over) to follow the sheep.

Cut the log house of felt or interfacing in five separate pieces, along the solid lines. You can then build it on the flannel board, from the bottom up. The rooster will perch on the roof to crow "cock-a-doodle-doo."

SHEEP

16

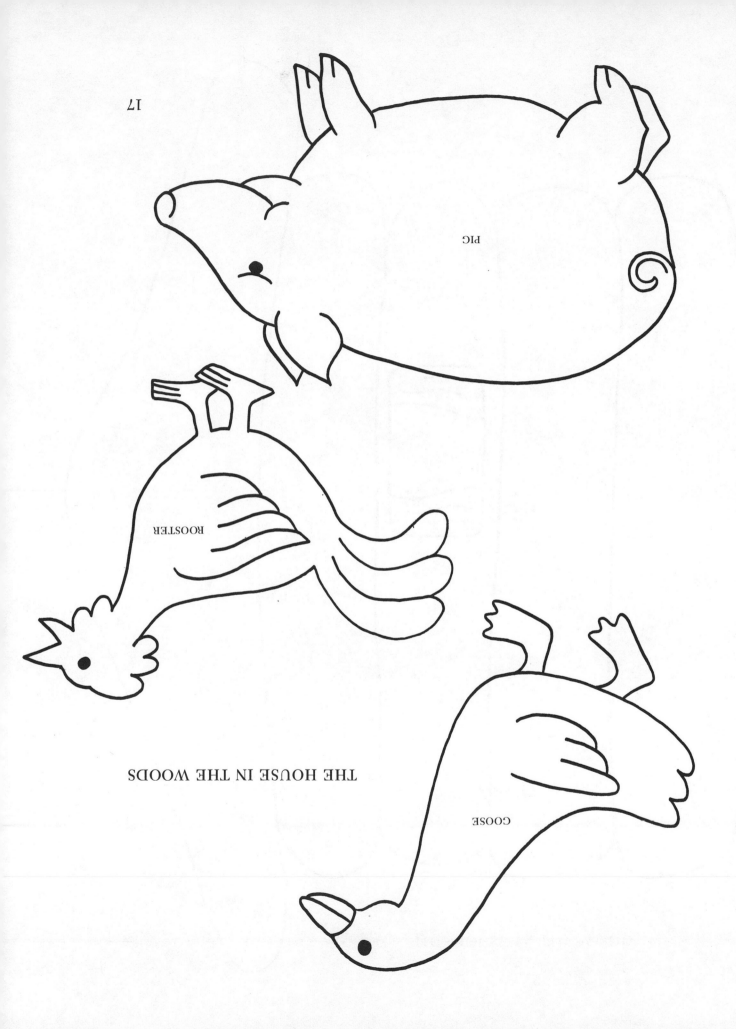

PIG

ROOSTER

THE HOUSE IN THE WOODS

GOOSE

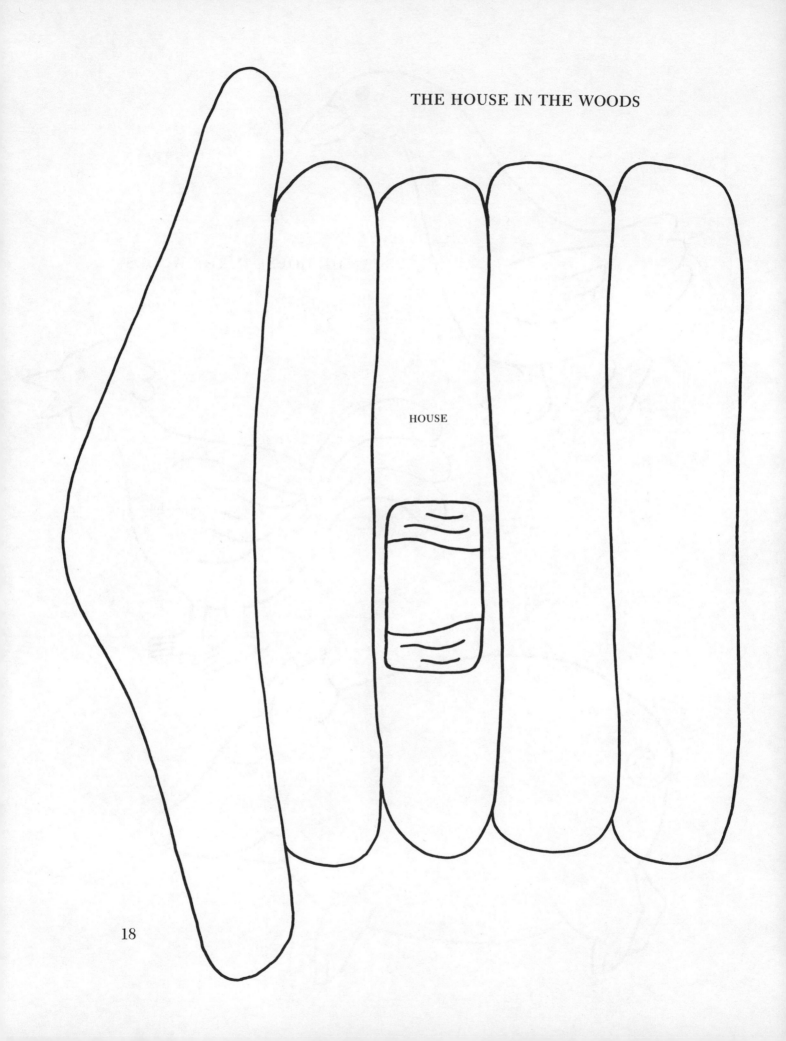

HOUSE

18

Hush, Little Baby

AN AMERICAN FOLK SONG

Hush lit-tle ba-by, don't say a word!

Pa-pa's gon-na buy you a mock-ing bird.

If that mocking bird won't sing,
Papa's gonna buy you a diamond ring.

If that diamond ring turns brass,
Papa's gonna buy you a looking glass.

If that looking glass gets broke,
Papa's gonna buy you a billy goat.

If that billy goat won't pull,
Papa's gonna buy you a cart and bull.

If that cart and bull turn over,
Papa's gonna buy you a dog named Rover.

19

If that dog named Rover won't bark,
Papa's gonna buy you a horse and cart.

If that horse and cart fall down,
You'll still be the sweetest little baby in town.

DIRECTIONS

Place the baby on the center left of the flannel board, and place all the other story figures, one by one, in a clockwise circle, ending with the toy horse and cart. You may want to actually turn the "cart and bull" and "horse and cart" figures upside-down at the appropriate times.

Participation

Distribute the story figures to the children, and let them come up and place them on the flannel board at the proper time in the song.

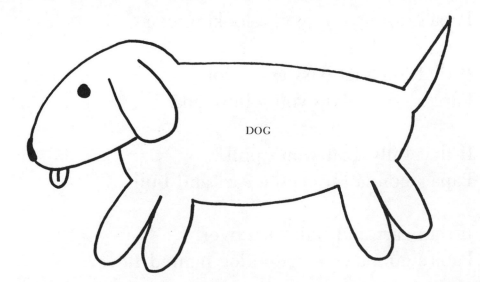

DOG

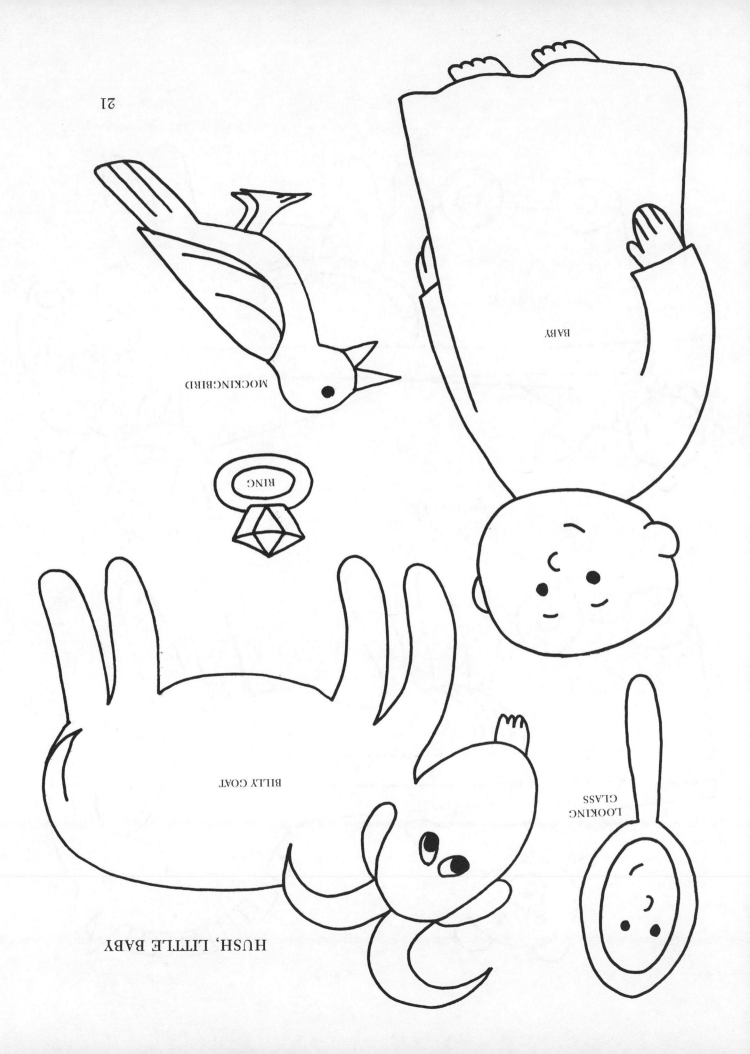

21

MOCKINGBIRD

BABY

RING

BILLY GOAT

LOOKING GLASS

HUSH, LITTLE BABY

HORSE AND CART

HUSH, LITTLE BABY

CART AND BULL

22

Old Mother Hubbard

A TRADITIONAL ENGLISH RHYME

(1)   Old Mother Hubbard
Went to the cupboard
   To get her poor dog a bone;
But when she got there
The cupboard was bare,
   And so the poor dog had none.

(2)   So she went to the baker's
   To buy him some bread,
But when she got back
   The poor dog was dead.

(3)   So she went to the undertaker's
   To buy him a coffin,
But when she came back
   The poor dog was laughin'.

(4)   So she took a clean dish
   To fetch him some tripe,
But when she came back
   He was smoking a pipe.

(5)   So she went to the tavern
   For white wine and red,
But when she came back
   The dog stood on his head.

(6) So she went to the alehouse
   To get him some beer,
  But when she came back
   The dog sat in a chair.

(7) So she went to the fruiterer's
   To buy him some fruit,
  But when she came back
   He was playing the flute.

(8) So she went to the cobbler's
   To buy him some shoes,
  But when she came back
   He was reading the news.

(9) So she went to the hosier's
   To buy him some hose,
  But when she came back
   He was dressed in his clothes.

(10) The dame made a curtsey,
   The dog made a bow;
  The dame said, "Your servant,"
   The dog said, "Bow wow!"

DIRECTIONS

Begin the rhyme with the cupboard at center, Mother Hubbard to the left, and the dog to the right. Even though the rhyme says that she went various places to do various things, you can just leave her on the flannel board (she was only gone a minute, and the focus is on the dog). The dog will be changed in position, or have something added to him, in almost every stanza. Pause after the words "when she came back . . ." to change the dog. It is better to make changes on the board during pauses than to make them while you are talking, so that your actions won't take attention away from your words.

Make the following changes on the flannel board for each stanza:

  (1) No change;
  (2) Place dog on back with feet up in the air;
  (3) Place dog standing up on back legs;
  (4) Place pipe in dog's mouth;
  (5) Remove pipe, turn him on his head;
  (6) Place dog in chair, sitting up;
  (7) Dog remains in chair—place flute in his mouth;
  (8) Remove flute, add newspaper;
  (9) Remove flute and chair, add clothes;
 (10) No change.

Follow-up

Lead a creative dramatics game in which you recite the poem and play the part of Mother Hubbard (or Father Hubbard).

Children sit at their desks or chairs, and all play the part of the dog simultaneously. Decide together how to mime the dog's actions, such as: ". . . and so the poor dog had none"—wail sadly; ". . . the dog stood on his head"—put head on desk, hands in the air; ". . . he was dressed in his clothes"—thumbs in shirt collar, smiling, looking sharp.

Recite the poem, turning your back on the group as you pretend to go to the baker's, undertaker's, etc. When you turn around to face the class again, on the words "but when she came back," the children must all be doing the correct mime for that stanza.

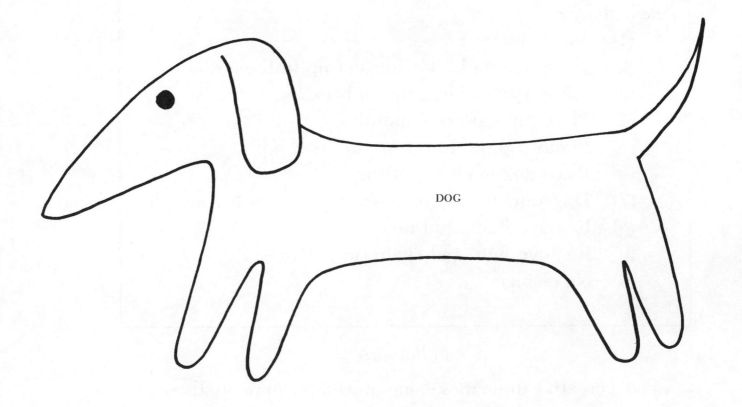

DOG

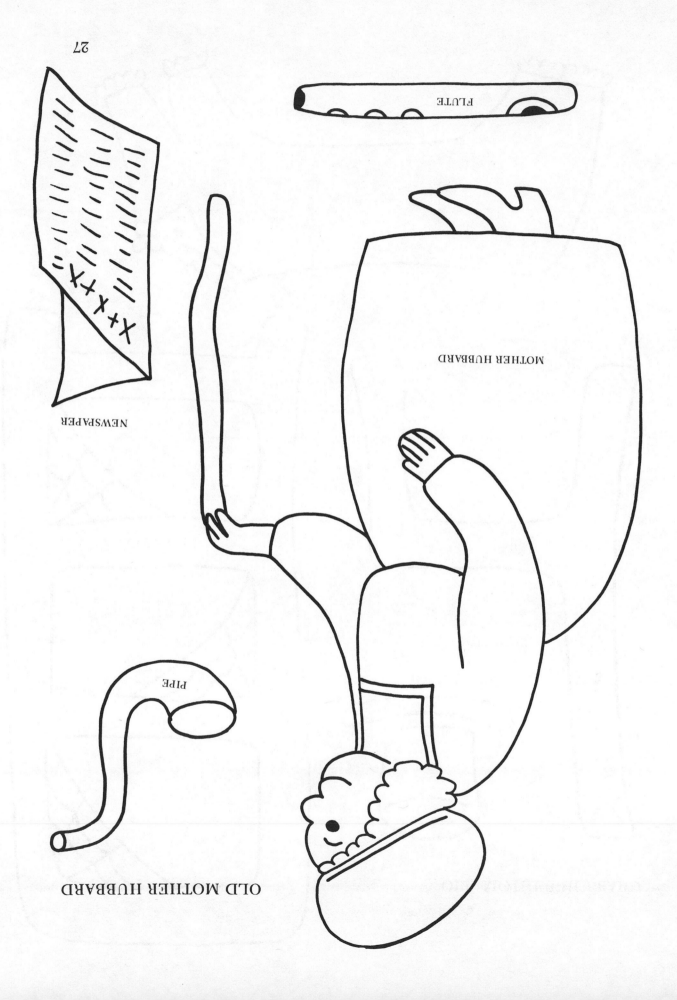

NEWSPAPER

FLUTE

MOTHER HUBBARD

PIPE

OLD MOTHER HUBBARD

OLD MOTHER HUBBARD

HAT

CUPBOARD

CHAIR

DOG CLOTHES

28

The Caterpillar

A POEM BY CHRISTINA ROSETTI

Brown and furry
Caterpillar, in a hurry
Take your walk
To the shady leaf or stalk
Or what not,
Which may be the chosen spot.
No toad spy you,
Hovering bird of prey pass by you;
Spin and die,
To live again as butterfly.

Participation

Children should be able to learn this short poem and say it along with you.

Follow-up

Use the figures to tell the life cycle of a caterpillar, and other caterpillar-to-butterfly stories.

DIRECTIONS

Cut the caterpillar and wings of felt. The wings are going to double as a chrysalis for the butterfly, so use an appropriate chrysalis color (tan or grey-green) for the wings. You can brighten up the butterfly side of the wings by gluing pieces of colored interfacing on that side.

Cut the toad and hawk from felt or interfacing. Before the children see the flannel board, place the toad at bottom right, and the hawk in upper center. The caterpillar goes at the center. After "No toad spy you . . ." remove the toad; after "Hovering bird of prey pass by you . . ." remove the hawk.

Have the wings prefolded, as on the dotted lines of the pattern, and place them over the caterpillar, as if he had made a chrysalis over himself. Then at the end of the poem, gently unfold the wings to reveal the butterfly.

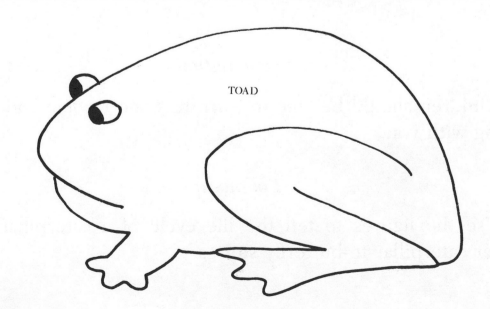

TOAD

30

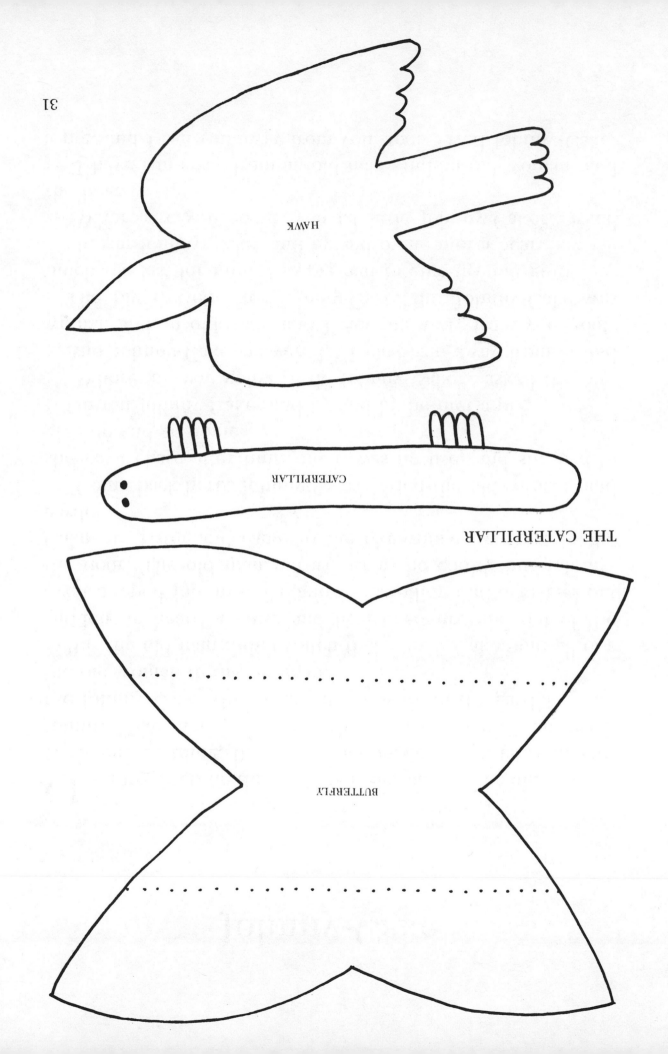

HAWK

CATERPILLAR

THE CATERPILLAR

BUTTERFLY

Johnny-Cake

AN ENGLISH TALE

ONCE UPON a time there lived an old man and an old woman. Early one morning, the old woman made a fine, fat, delicious Johnny-Cake, and put it into the oven to bake. "You watch the Johnny-Cake while I go out and work in the garden," said the old woman to the old man.

But the old man didn't watch the Johnny-Cake, and all of a sudden he heard a noise and he looked up, and out of the oven popped Johnny-Cake and went rolling end-over-end out the door. The old man ran as fast as he could, but Johnny-Cake ran faster and came to the old woman working in the garden.

"Come back here, Johnny-Cake!" cried the old woman, and she gave chase after him, but it was no use, and she had to give up and go home.

On ran Johnny-Cake, and by and by he met a pig.

"Where are you going, little Johnny-Cake?" asked the pig.

And Johnny-Cake answered, "I have run away from an old woman and an old man, and I can run away from you, too!"

The pig trotted after Johnny-Cake, but Johnny-Cake was much too fast for him. The pig had to give up and go home.

On ran Johnny-Cake, and by and by he met a bear.

"Where are you going, you fat little Johnny-Cake?" asked the bear.

"I have run away from an old man, and an old woman, and a pig, and I can run away from you, too!" cried Johnny-Cake.

The bear ran after Johnny-Cake, but Johnny-Cake ran faster, never stopping to look behind him, and the bear had to give up.

On went Johnny-Cake, and by and by he came to a wolf.

"Where are you going, you sweet little Johnny-Cake?" asked the wolf.

"I have run away from an old man, and an old woman, and a pig, and a bear, and I can run away from you, too!" sang Johnny-Cake.

"Oh you can, can you?" snarled the wolf, and he set out after Johnny-Cake, who ran and ran without ever looking back. The wolf saw there was no hope of catching Johnny-Cake, and he gave up.

On went Johnny-Cake, and by and by he came to a fox lying by the side of the road. "Where are you going, dear little Johnny-Cake?" asked the fox.

"I've run away from an old man, and an old woman, and a pig, and a bear, and a wolf, and I can run away from you, too!"

"What's that you say, Johnny-Cake? I didn't hear you," said the fox. "Come a little closer."

Johnny-Cake moved a tiny bit closer to the fox and said, "I have run away from an old man, and an old woman, and a pig, and a bear, and a wolf, and I can run away from you, too!"

"Oh, my poor old ears. I still can't hear a single word. Please come just a little bit closer," said the fox.

Johnny-Cake came right up to the fox's ear and shouted out, "I've run away from an old man, and an old woman, and a pig, and a bear, and a wolf, and I can. . . ."

But that was all he said, for the fox snapped him up and

swallowed him in the twinkling of an eye. And that was the end of Johnny-Cake.

DIRECTIONS

Set up the flannel board with the oven in the center and the man and woman on either side of it. The oven can be made of interfacing or felt. If you are using felt, use a suitable color for the oven and glue on flames of orange or red. Johnny-Cake is placed in the oven at the appropriate time, and, when he rolls out the door, first he, then the old man, then the oven are taken off the flannel board.

Next, place Johnny-Cake at the center of the flannel board. He will stay there as he meets the woman, then the various animals, which are placed on alternating sides of him. Johnny-Cake will not move, except in the audience's imagination, until the end, when he gets closer and closer to the fox. Be sure you place the fox at the very edge, or in a far corner, of the flannel board, so that Johnny-Cake will have room to travel to get to him. Grab the story figure of Johnny-Cake quickly and keep him in your closed hand when the fox snaps him up and swallows him.

Participation

As the group learns the story, have individual children take parts and say the words of the characters while you narrate and move the figures on the flannel board.

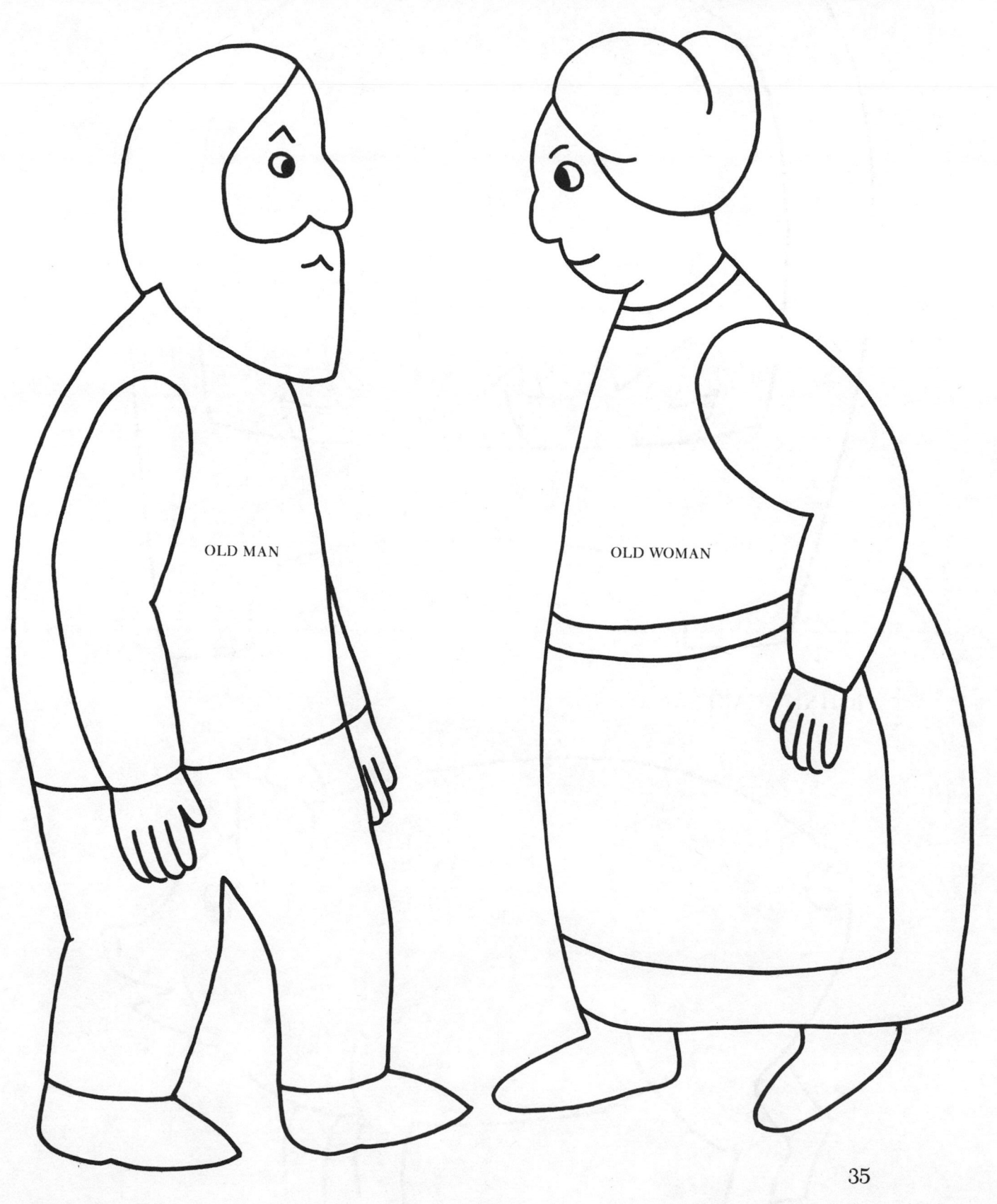

OLD MAN

OLD WOMAN

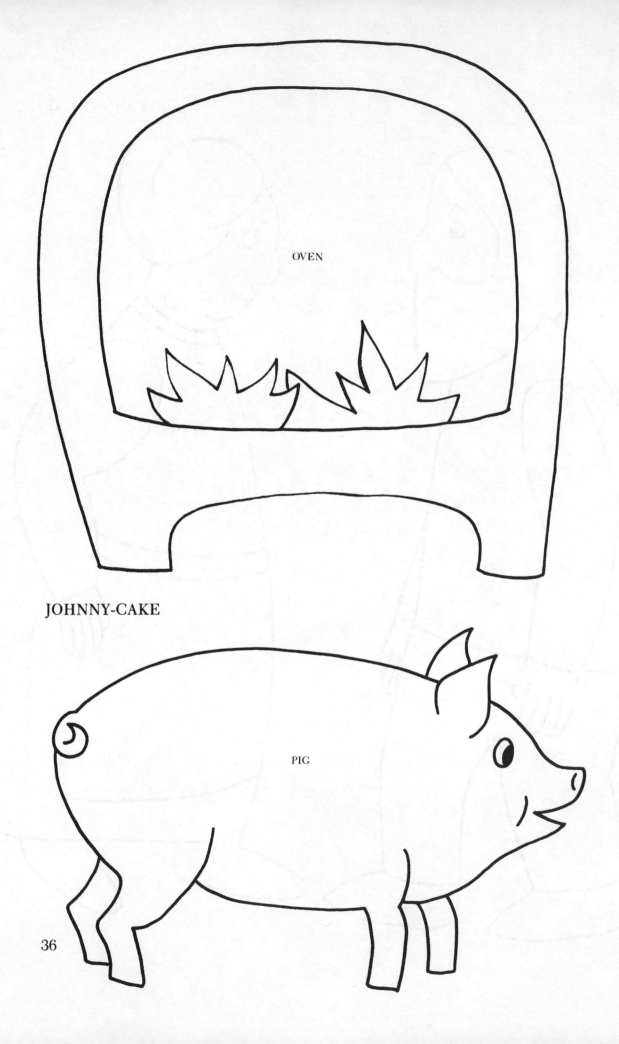

OVEN

JOHNNY-CAKE

PIG

36

JOHNNY-CAKE

BEAR

38

This Is the House That Jack Built

AN ENGLISH TALE

THIS IS the house that Jack built.

This is the malt that lay in the house that Jack built.

This is the rat, that ate the malt, that lay in the house that Jack built.

This is the cat, that killed the rat, that ate the malt, that lay in the house that Jack built.

This is the dog, that worried the cat, that killed the rat, that ate the malt, that lay in the house that Jack built.

This is the cow with the crumpled horn, that tossed the dog, that worried the cat, that killed the rat, that ate the malt, that lay in the house that Jack built.

This is the maiden all forlorn, that milked the cow with the crumpled horn, that tossed the dog, that worried the cat, that killed the rat, that ate the malt, that lay in the house that Jack built.

This is the man all tattered and torn, that kissed the maiden all forlorn, that milked the cow with the crumpled horn, that tossed the dog, that worried the cat, that killed the rat, that ate the malt, that lay in the house that Jack built.

This is the priest all shaven and shorn, that married the man all tattered and torn, that kissed the maiden all forlorn, that milked the cow with the crumpled horn, that tossed the dog, that worried the cat, that killed the rat, that ate the malt, that lay in the house that Jack built.

This is the cock that crowed in the morn, that wakened the

priest all shaven and shorn, that married the man all tattered and torn, that kissed the maiden all forlorn, that milked the cow with the crumpled horn, that tossed the dog, that worried the cat, that killed the rat, that ate the malt, that lay in the house that Jack built.

This is the farmer sowing his corn, that kept the cock that crowed in the morn, that wakened the priest all shaven and shorn, that married the man all tattered and torn, that kissed the maiden all forlorn, that milked the cow with the crumpled horn, that tossed the dog, that worried the cat, that killed the rat, that ate the malt, that lay in the house that Jack built.

DIRECTIONS

Make a house, about five inches square, at the top center of the flannel board (follow the directions in "Making Story Figures for the Flannel Board," pp. 5–6). As you tell the story, place the malt, then the rat, inside the house. Then place the other story figures outside the house in a counterclockwise circle, beginning at the left side of the house, so that at the end of the story the cock can roost on the right-hand side of the roof, and the farmer stands just to the right of the house.

Participation

The rhythm and repetition of the story make children want to say it along with you, and you should encourage this. After you have told it several times with a group, ask for volunteers to go through one whole sequence each, beginning with the newest story character added and ending with "that lay in the house that Jack built."

Follow-up

The story can be acted out in pantomime by a group of nine or ten (number ten would play the malt), with you narrating. Each character has a short bit of pantomime he or she can perform as you pause in the narration: "This is the farmer sowing his corn (pause for action), that. . . ." Some of the actions are potentially violent, such as the cat killing the rat and the cow tossing the dog. Tell the children they cannot touch each other during the pantomime: the cat acts fierce while the rat falls dead, the cow—two finger-horns on her head—makes a tossing motion as the dog jumps, etc.

COW

RAT

COCK

MALT

THE HOUSE THAT JACK BUILT

FORLORN
MAIDEN

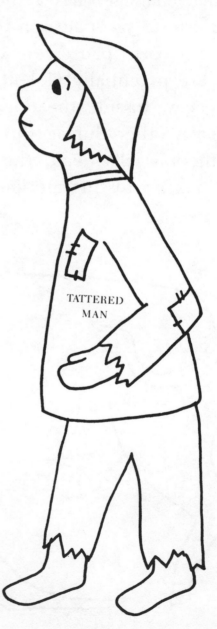

TATTERED
MAN

42

THE HOUSE THAT JACK BUILT

43

ARCADIA PUBLIC LIBRARY
ARCADIA, WISCONSIN 54612

The Three Billy Goats

A NORWEGIAN TALE

ONCE UPON a time, a long, long time age, three billy goats lived on the side of a mountain. The day came when they had eaten up every bit of grass on that mountain, and they had to look for a new place to live. They saw that the next mountain was covered with fresh green grass; but on the way to that mountain there was a river, and across the river there was a bridge, and under that bridge there lived a horrid old troll, with eyes as big as saucers and a nose as long as a poker.

First it was the turn of the smallest billy goat to cross the bridge. "Trip, trap, trip, trap" was the sound of his hooves on the bridge.

"Who is that tripping over my bridge?" roared the troll.

"It is the smallest billy goat."

"Now I am coming to eat you up!" cried the troll, and with that he jumped up onto the bridge.

"Oh, no, please don't eat me up! I have a brother coming along, and he is so much bigger and fatter than I am that you really should wait and eat him," said the smallest billy goat.

"Bigger? Fatter? Oh, very well, be off with you!" shouted the troll, and he jumped back under the bridge. The little billy goat trotted across the bridge and up onto the grassy mountain.

Next, it was the turn of the medium-sized billy goat. "Trip, trap, trip, trap" was the sound of his hooves on the bridge.

"Who is that tripping over my bridge?" roared the troll.

"It is the medium-sized billy goat."

44

"Now I am coming to eat you up!" cried the troll, and with that, he jumped up onto the bridge.

"Oh, no, please don't eat me up!" said the medium-sized billy goat. "I have a bigger brother coming along, and he is so much juicier and tastier than I am that you really should wait and eat him."

"Juicier? Tastier? Oh, very well, be off with you!" shouted the troll, and he jumped back under the bridge. The medium-sized billy goat trotted across the bridge and up onto the grassy mountain.

Next it was the turn of the biggest billy goat: "trip, trap, trip, trap." The sound of his hooves made the bridge tremble and shake.

"Who is that tripping over my bridge?" roared the troll.

"It is the biggest billy goat!" roared the big goat in a great big voice of his own.

"Now I am coming to eat you up!" cried the troll, and he jumped up onto the bridge.

"Oh no you don't," said the goat:

"For on my head I have two spears
And I'll poke your eyeballs out your ears!
And on my feet I have two great stones
And I'll grind you to bits, body and bones!"

The biggest billy goat butted the troll up into the air. When the troll came down, he was smashed to pieces, and that was the end of him.

Then the big billy goat trotted over the bridge and up the mountain to join his brothers. They ate, and ate, and ate, and they got very fat. And if the fat hasn't rolled off them, why, they're still fat, so

Snip, snap, snout
This tale is told out!

DIRECTIONS

Cut two triangular mountains of felt, approximately 7″ wide by 9″ high, one brown and one green. Place the brown mountain in the lower left of the flannel board, the green mountain in the upper right, with the bridge joining the two.

Begin the story with the goats on the brown mountain: big goat at the bottom, medium-sized goat on top of him, smallest goat at the very top. The troll is under the bridge. At the cues in the story, place the troll on the bridge, then back under the bridge. The goats will end up on the green mountain in positions identical to their original positions on the brown mountain.

Participation

The audience always enjoys adding the goats' "trip-traps"—either by saying the words along with you or by stomping their feet. When the group knows the story well, choose four children to speak the parts of the characters while you provide the narration and move the figures on the board.

Follow-up

This story is perfect for acting out with simple puppets or in pantomime. During the acting out, you can still provide the narration if the children are too young to carry the story by themselves.

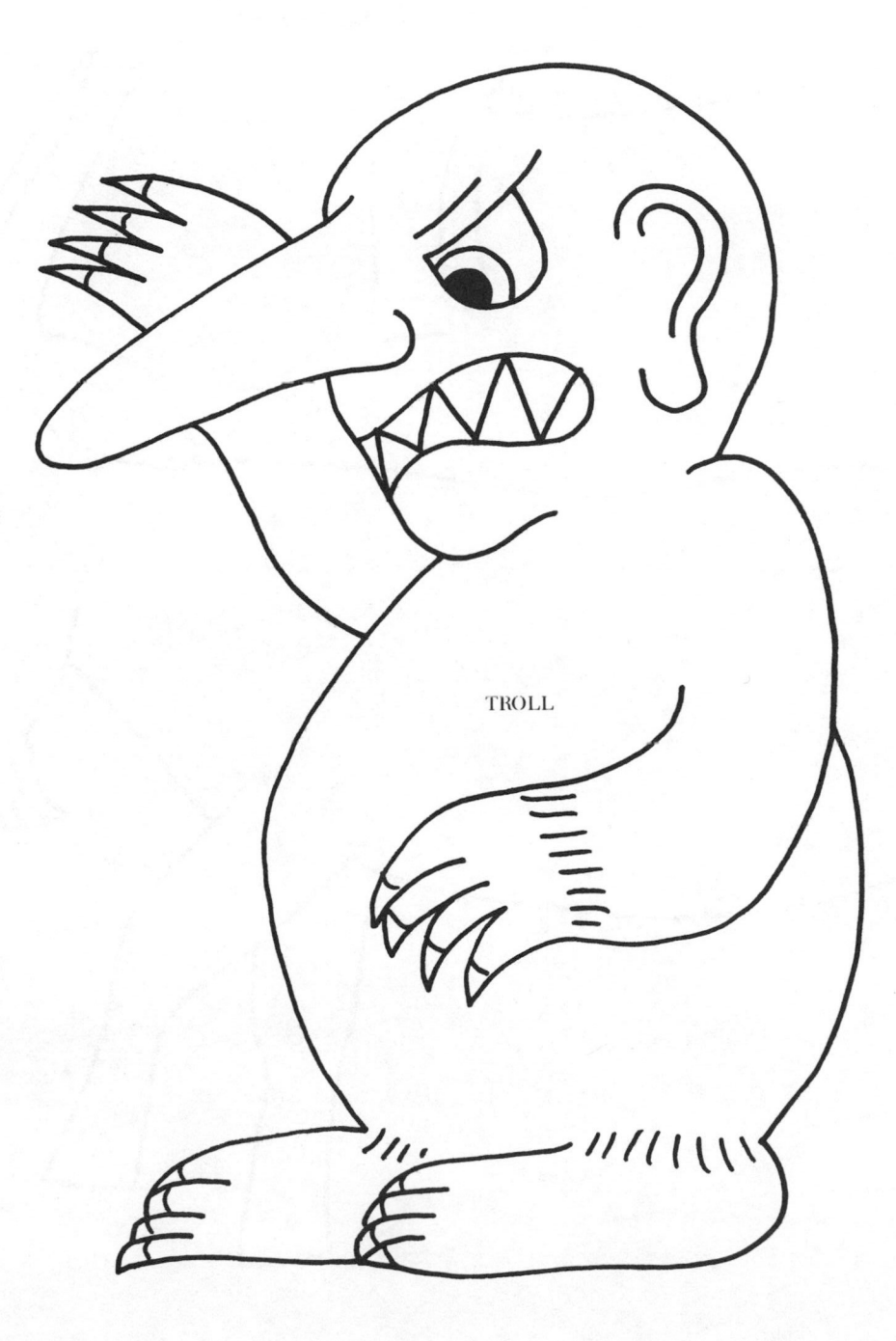

TROLL

THE THREE BILLY GOATS

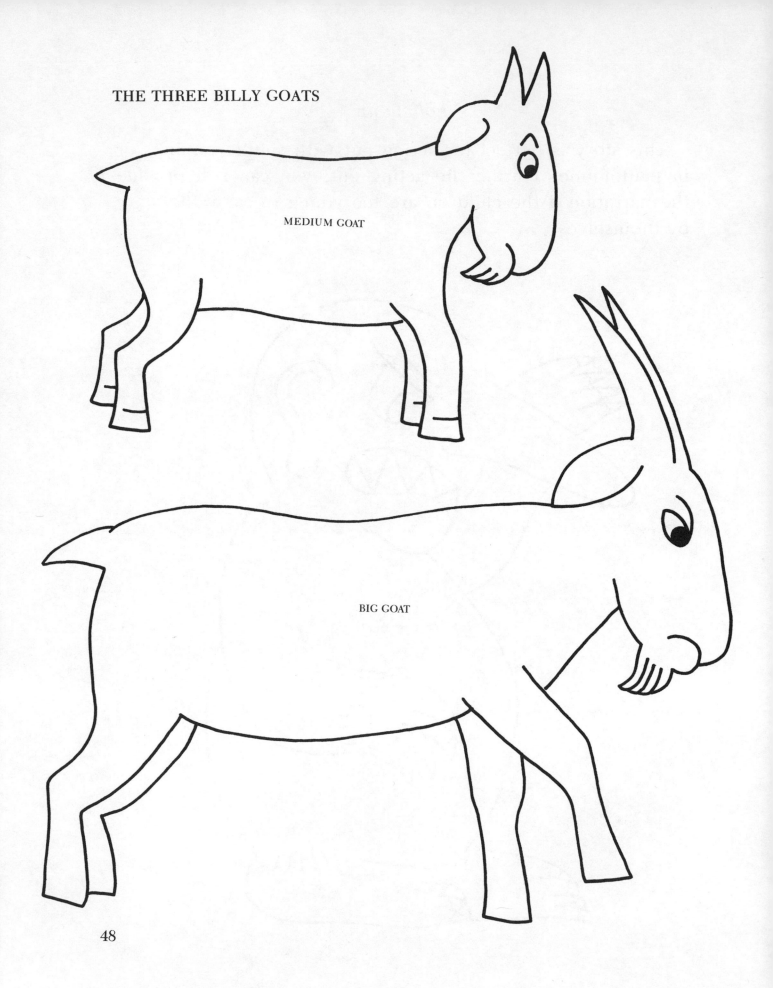

MEDIUM GOAT

BIG GOAT

48

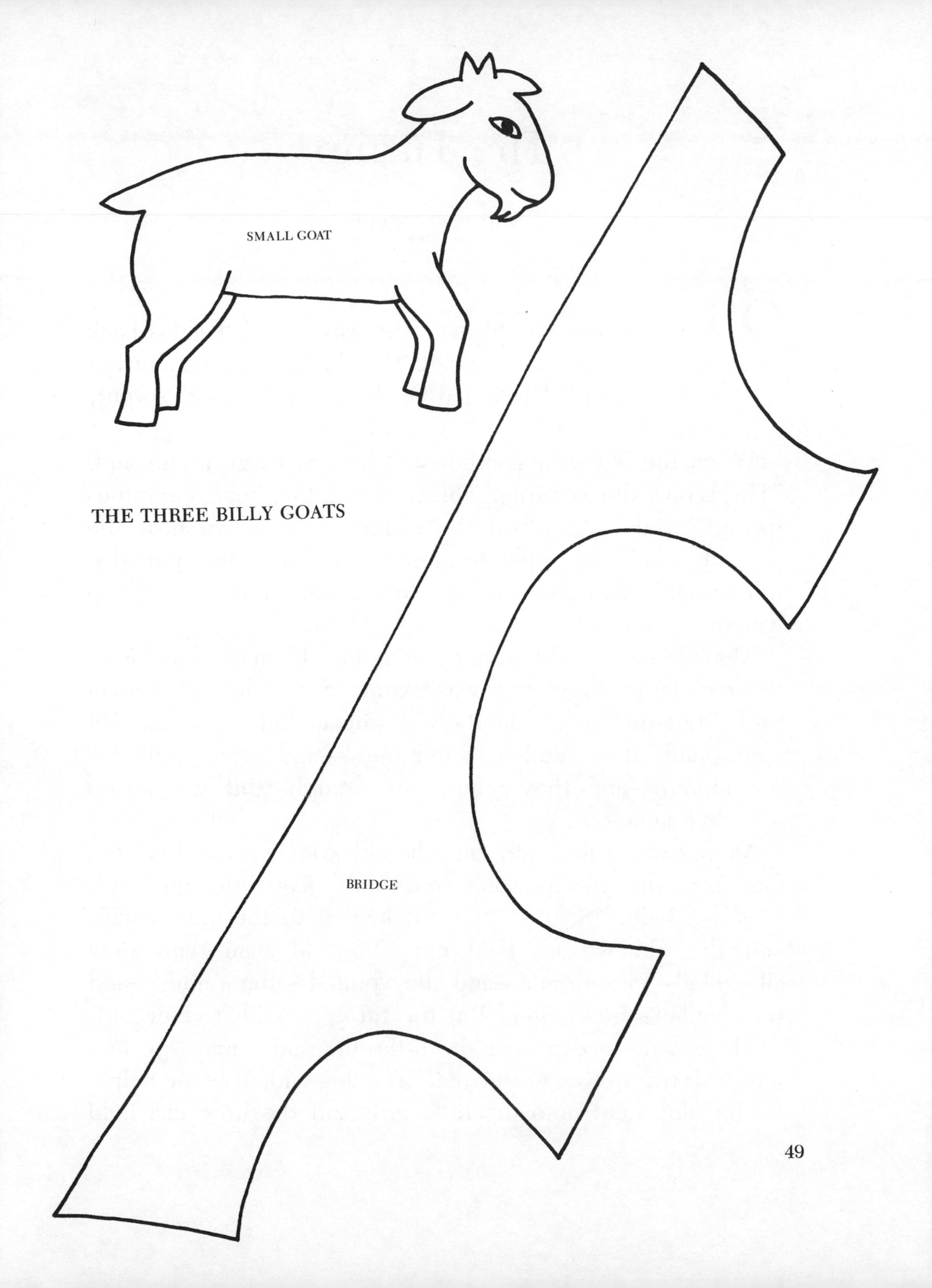

SMALL GOAT

THE THREE BILLY GOATS

BRIDGE

49

The Turnip

A RUSSIAN TALE

Once there was an old man—he was so old that his back went crick-crack when he walked. The old man planted a turnip seed in the ground. He waited for the green leaves to sprout, first a little, then a lot.

When the old man saw how tall the leaves grew, he said, "This is no ordinary turnip! This is a great, big, huge, enormous turnip!" And he grabbed the turnip leaves down near the ground, and he pulled—mmmmmh!—and he pulled—mmmmmh!—and he pulled—mmmmmh! But the turnip wouldn't come out.

Along came an old woman, and the old man said, "Fee, fie, foe, fout, this turnip won't come out!" The old woman said, "Let me help." So the old woman held onto the old man, and they pulled—mmmmmh!—and they pulled—mmmmmh!—and they pulled—mmmmmh! But the turnip wouldn't come out.

Along came a little girl, and the old woman said, "Fee, fie, foe, fout, this turnip won't come out!" The little girl said, "Let me help." So the little girl held onto the old woman, and the old woman held onto the old man, and they all pulled—mmmmmh!—and they pulled—mmmmmh!—and they pulled—mmmmmh! But the turnip wouldn't come out.

Along came a dog, and the little girl said, "Fee, fie, foe, fout, this turnip won't come out!" The dog said, "Let me help." So the dog held onto the little girl, and the little girl held

50

onto the old woman, and the old woman held onto the old man, and they pulled—mmmmmh!—and they pulled—mmmmmh!—and they pulled—mmmmmh! But the turnip wouldn't come out.

Along came a cat, and the dog said, "Fee, fie, foe, fout, this turnip won't come out!" The cat said, "Let me help." So the cat held onto the dog, and the dog held onto the little girl, and the little girl held onto the old woman, and the old woman held onto the old man, and they pulled—mmmmmh!—and they pulled—mmmmmh!—and they pulled—mmmmmh! But the turnip wouldn't come out.

Along came a mouse, and the cat said, "Fee, fie, foe, fout, this turnip won't come out." The mouse said, "Let me help." "Ha, ha, ha!" laughed the cat. "What help can a little mouse be?"

"You never know," said the mouse. So the mouse held onto the cat, and the cat held onto the dog, and the dog held onto the little girl, and the little girl held onto the old woman, and the old woman held onto the old man, and they all pulled—mmmmmh!—and they pulled—mmmmmh!—and they pulled—mmmmmh!—AND THE TURNIP CAME OUT!

And sure enough, it *was* a great, big, huge, enormous turnip!

Participation

The children can help you as you mime pulling hard—mmmmmh!—on the turnip. After the turnip comes out, they can share ideas about what the people and animals might do with such an enormous turnip.

DIRECTIONS

Cut the turnip leaves from green felt and the turnip from white felt, coloring the top area with a purple marker. Then glue the two together with fabric glue. Cut the large, oblong-shaped ground of brown felt, or of a color to match the flannel board.

"Plant" the turnip on the far right-hand side of the flannel board before the children see it. Fold the leaves down, then fold the middle leaf back up so that the leaf-tip is just above the turnip. Cover the turnip with the ground piece so that the upturned leaf-tip is just below the small hump in the ground (this shows you where to reach in to pull it up when the time comes in the story). Then pin all four corners of the ground to the flannel board with straight pins (or safety pins, concealed under the felt, if you are worried about the children getting to them).

When the turnip begins to sprout, reach just under the small hump in the ground and pull the tip of the middle leaf out where the children can see it (on "first a little"), then pull up all the leaves—but *not* the turnip (on "then a lot").

As each new story character enters, place it by itself at the left side of the flannel board. On the words "held onto," move it over so that its arm overlaps the previous character's figure.

Pull the turnip out from under the ground piece on the very last pull, and place it on the flannel board for everyone to see.

Follow-up

"The Turnip" is extraordinarily fun to act out! Everyone can help plant and water the seed. Then you can play the part of turnip and narrator as the child playing the old man pulls on your clasped hands. Add woman, children, cats, dogs, and finally mice, so that everyone is included, to the line of pullers. Finally, as the turnip, you can pop out (stand up).

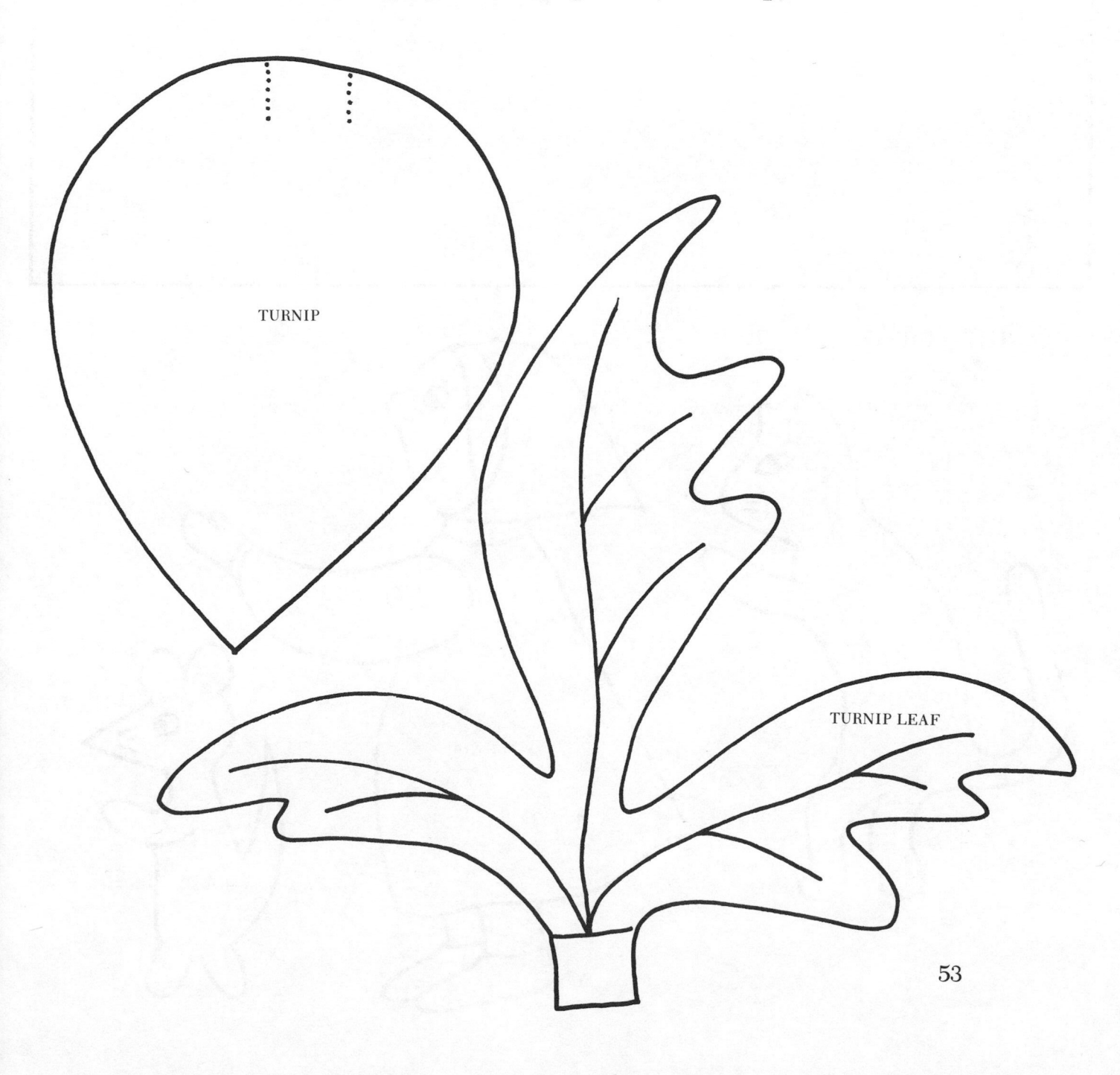

TURNIP

TURNIP LEAF

53

GROUND

THE TURNIP

CAT

LITTLE GIRL

MOUSE

54

OLD WOMAN

OLD MAN

DOG

Henny Penny

AN ENGLISH TALE

ONE DAY Henny Penny was pecking corn in the cornyard when—whack!—something hit her on the head. "Goodness gracious me!" said Henny Penny. "The sky's a-going to fall. I must go and tell the king."

So she went along, and she went along, and she went along, till she met Cocky Locky. "Where are you going, Henny Penny?" asked Cocky Locky.

"Oh! I'm going to tell the king the sky's a-falling," said Henny Penny.

"May I come with you?" asked Cocky Locky.

"Certainly," said Henny Penny. So Henny Penny and Cocky Locky went to tell the king the sky was a-falling.

They went along, and they went along, and they went along, till they met Ducky Daddles. "Where are you going, Henny Penny and Cocky Locky?" asked Ducky Daddles.

"Oh! We're going to tell the king the sky's a-falling," said Henny Penny and Cocky Locky.

"May I come with you?" asked Ducky Daddles.

"Certainly," said Henny Penny and Cocky Locky. So Henny Penny, Cocky Locky, and Ducky Daddles went to tell the king the sky was a-falling.

So they went along, and they went along, and they went along, till they met Goosey Poosey. "Where are you going, Henny Penny, Cocky Locky, and Ducky Daddles?" asked Goosey Poosey.

"Oh! We're going to tell the king the sky's a-falling," said Henny Penny and Cocky Locky and Ducky Daddles.

"May I come with you?" asked Goosey Poosey.

"Certainly!" said Henny Penny, Cocky Locky, and Ducky Daddles. So Henny Penny, Cocky Locky, Ducky Daddles, and Goosey Poosey went to tell the king the sky was a-falling.

So they went along, and they went along, and they went along, till they met Turkey Lurkey. "Where are you going, Henny Penny, Cocky Locky, Ducky Daddles, and Goosey Poosey?" asked Turkey Lurkey.

"Oh! We're going to tell the king the sky's a-falling," said Henny Penny, Cocky Locky, Ducky Daddles, and Goosey Poosey.

"May I come with you, Henny Penny, Cocky Locky, Ducky Daddles, and Goosey Poosey?" asked Turkey Lurkey.

"Oh, certainly, Turkey Lurkey," said Henny Penny, Cocky Locky, Ducky Daddles, and Goosey Poosey. So Henny Penny, Cocky Locky, Ducky Daddles, Goosey Poosey, and Turkey Lurkey all went to tell the king the sky was a-falling.

So they went along, and they went along, and they went along, till they met Foxy Loxy, and Foxy Loxy said to Henny Penny, Cocky Locky, Ducky Daddles, Goosey Poosey, and Turkey Lurkey, "Where are you going, Henny Penny, Cocky Locky, Ducky Daddles, Goosey Poosey, and Turkey Lurkey?"

And Henny Penny, Cocky Locky, Ducky Daddles, Goosey Poosey, and Turkey Lurkey said to Foxy Loxy, "We're going to tell the king that the sky's a-falling."

"Then you will certainly want to use this shortcut," said Foxy Loxy. "Follow me!" And Foxy Loxy went into his den. Henny Penny, Cocky Locky, Ducky Daddles, Goosey Poosey, and Turkey Lurkey did not like the idea of going into such a dark cave, but finally Turkey Lurkey went in. And Goosey Poosey went in. And Ducky Daddles went in. And Cocky Locky went in.

"Cock-a-doodle-doo!" cried Cocky Locky. "Run, Henny Penny, run! Foxy Loxy will eat you. . . ."

Henny Penny ran all the way home, and she never did get to tell the king that the sky was a-falling.

DIRECTIONS

Color these story figures on both sides. Cut a four-inch circle of black or brown felt to represent Foxy Loxy's den and place it at the upper right-hand corner of the flannel board before you begin the story. The birds walk along a diagonal line running from lower left to upper right of the flannel board. Place Henny Penny about six inches from the den, facing right. She will remain there for most of the story. As she meets each character, place it to her right, facing her. When each decides to follow her, flip the piece over and place it behind her, to her left. Take Foxy Loxy and each of the birds off the board as they go into his den.

Follow-up

The silly names and repetition in this story make it delightfully humorous for young children. Some teachers and parents object to the realistic ending, yet the lesson is an important one: uncritical acceptance of what others say, and going along with the crowd, can lead to disaster. In acting out this story, after hearing it, children can improvise other endings in which the characters manage to escape being eaten by Foxy Loxy.

59

GOOSEY POOSEY

DUCKY DADDLES

HENNY PENNY

COCKY LOCKY

HENNY PENNY

TURKEY LURKEY

ACORN

FOXY LOXY

Bingo

AN AMERICAN FOLK SONG

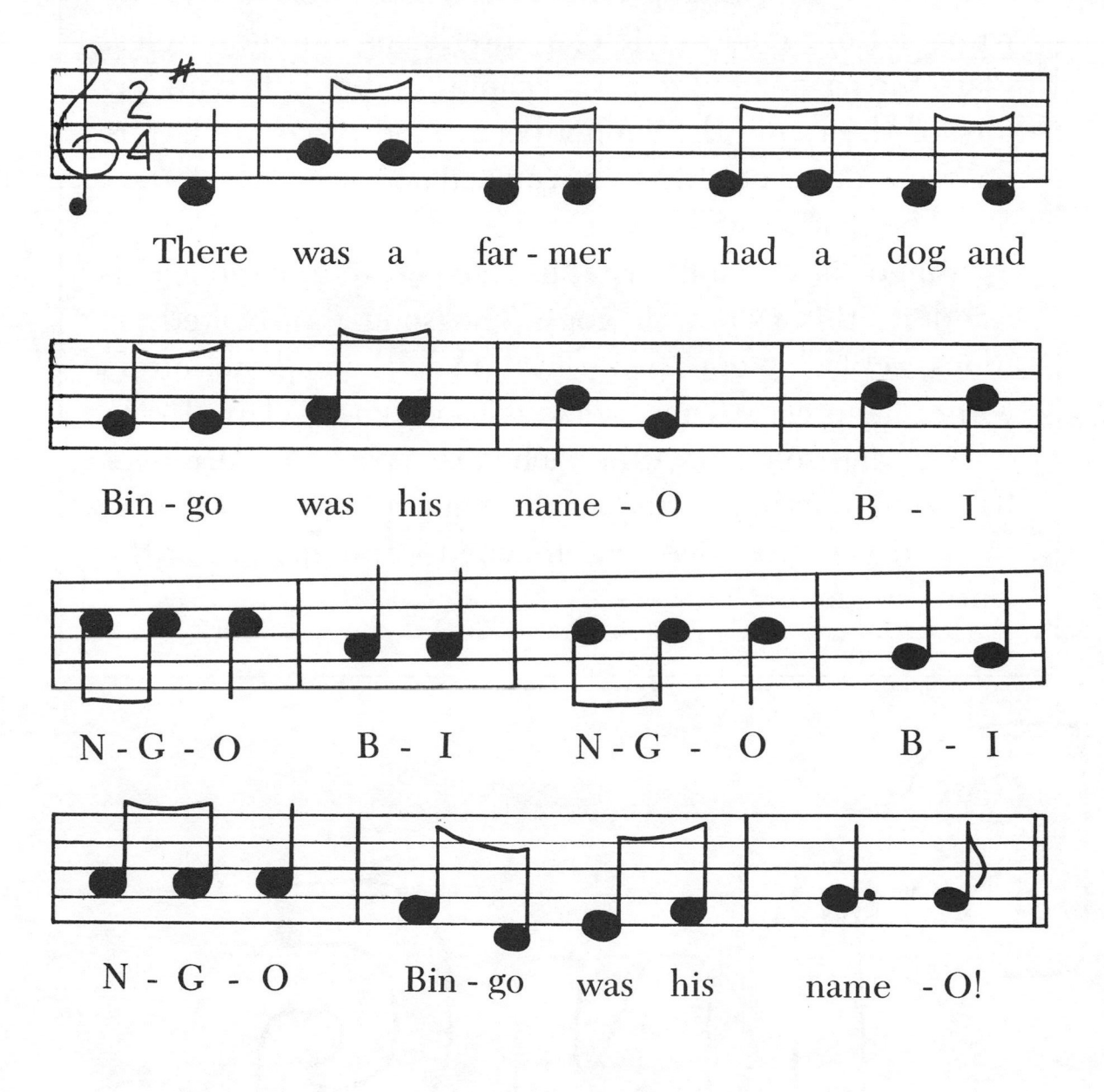

There was a far-mer had a dog and

Bin-go was his name-O   B - I

N-G - O   B - I   N-G - O   B - I

N - G - O   Bin-go was his   name - O!

Participation

This easily learned song is very infectious; in no time at all
you can have your whole group joining in.

DIRECTIONS

To make the letters, cut out red felt circles and glue white letters made of felt or interfacing on the circles. Place the farmer and the dog, leaning on her left shoulder, toward the top of the flannel board, and place the letters below, spelling out BINGO. You will be turning the letters over, beginning with "B."

"Bingo" is an old favorite; in case you've never encountered it, this is how it goes: The song is repeated six times, replacing one, two, three, four, then all the letters with a hand clap. Thus, verse two becomes "clap - I - N - G - O," and so forth. After each verse, pause to turn over the corresponding letter on the flannel board, so that at the end you have five red circles in a row instead of the word "bingo."

BINGO

CIRCLE

FARMER

BINGO

63

The Goat in the Turnip Field

A NORWEGIAN TALE

ONE AFTERNOON, a little boy was tending his turnip field when the big billy goat came along and began eating the tasty tops of all the turnips. The boy shouted at the goat, "Get out of my turnip field!" He pulled the goat, and he pushed the goat, but the goat would not stop eating the turnips. So the poor boy began to cry.

Along came the fox, who asked the boy why he was crying.

"The billy goat got into the turnip field, and he's eating all our turnips, and he won't stop," sobbed the boy.

So the fox went over to the turnip field to try and bite the billy goat's leg to make him run away, but the billy goat butted the fox with his horns—BOOM!—and tossed the fox up in the air, and the fox landed next to the boy, and now they were both crying.

Along came the wolf, who asked why the boy and the fox were crying.

"The billy goat got into the turnip field, and he's eating all the boy's turnips, and he won't stop," sobbed the fox.

So the wolf went over to the turnip field and growled at the billy goat to scare him away. But the billy goat just butted the wolf with his horns—BOOM!—and tossed the wolf up in the air, and the wolf landed next to the boy and the fox, and now all three of them were crying.

Along came the bear, who asked why the boy and the fox and the wolf were crying.

"The billy goat got into the boy's turnip field, and he's eating all the turnips, and he won't stop," sobbed the wolf.

So the bear went over to the turnip field to spank the billy goat with his claws and make him go away. But the billy goat just butted the bear with his horns—BOOM!—and tossed the bear up into the air, and the bear landed next to the boy and the fox and the wolf, and now all four of them were crying.

Along came the bumble bee, who asked why the boy and the fox and the wolf and the bear were all crying.

"The billy goat got into the turnip field, and he's eating all the boy's turnips, and he won't stop," sobbed the bear.

So the bumble bee flew into the turnip field—BUZZ!—and landed on the billy goat's back leg, and stung him a great huge sting—YOW!—and the billy goat got out of that turnip field so fast nobody saw him leave, and the boy and the fox and the wolf and the bear all stopped crying.

DIRECTIONS

Place the turnips in the upper left of the flannel board with just enough room to their left for the billy goat. Place the boy to the right of the turnips and begin the story. When the boy begins to cry, move him to the lower left of the flannel board. As each helpful animal comes along, it sits to the right of the boy (or previous animal), then goes up next to the billy goat, then—BOOM!—returns to sit and cry next to the others. When the bee flies into the garden, build suspense by "flying" it toward the goat's back leg slowly while making a buzzing noise and holding the bee between your thumb and forefinger so that the children can see it.

Participation

Children can participate vocally in the story, once they have heard it, by saying "BOOM!", "BUZZ", "YOW!," and "boo-hoo-hoo" at the appropriate times.

Follow-up

Use the patterns to make stick puppets from heavy paper and perform the story as a play, using the flannel board or a cardboard box as the stage.

BEAR

BILLY GOAT

THE GOAT IN THE TURNIP FIELD

WOLF

LITTLE BOY

67

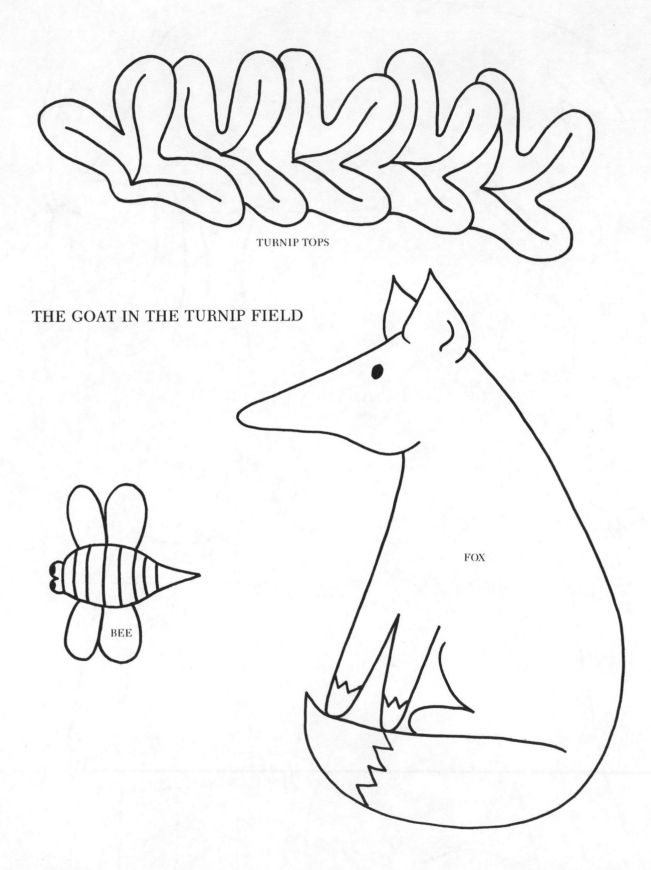

TURNIP TOPS

THE GOAT IN THE TURNIP FIELD

BEE

FOX

The Old Woman and Her Pig

AN ENGLISH TALE

A WOMAN was sweeping her yard, and she found a crooked sixpence on the ground. "What good luck," says she. "I can go to market and buy me a little pig."

So she went to market and bought herself a fine, fat little piggy. As she was bringing it home, she came to a stile,† but the piggy wouldn't go over it. Oh, she pushed and she pulled at the pig, but it just wouldn't go over that stile.

The woman went a ways, and she found a dog, and said to him, "Dog! Dog! Bite pig! Piggy won't jump over the stile and I'll never get home tonight." But the dog would not.

She went a little further, and she met a stick, and she said, "Stick! Stick! Beat dog! Dog won't bite pig, piggy won't jump over the stile, and I'll never get home tonight." But the stick would not.

She went a little further, and she met some fire, and she said, "Fire! Fire! Burn stick! Stick won't beat dog, dog won't bite pig, piggy won't jump over the stile, and I'll never get home tonight." But the fire would not.

She went a little further, and she met some water, and she said, "Water! Water! Quench fire! Fire won't burn stick, stick won't beat dog, dog won't bite pig, piggy won't jump over the stile, and I'll never get home tonight." But the water would not.

She went a little further, and she met an ox, and she said, "Ox! Ox! Drink water! Water won't quench fire, fire won't

† A set of steps or stairs to climb over a fence or wall.

burn stick, stick won't beat dog, dog won't bite pig, piggy won't jump over the stile, and I'll never get home tonight." But the ox would not.

She went a little further, and she met a butcher, and she said, "Butcher! Butcher! Kill ox! Ox won't drink water, water won't quench fire, fire won't burn stick, stick won't beat dog, dog won't bite pig, piggy won't jump over the stile, and I'll never get home tonight." But the butcher would not.

She went a little further, and she met a rope, and she said: "Rope! Rope! Whip butcher! Butcher won't kill ox, ox won't drink water, water won't quench fire, fire won't burn stick, stick won't beat dog, dog won't bite pig, piggy won't jump over the stile, and I'll never get home tonight." But the rope would not.

She went a little further, and she met a rat, and she said, "Rat! Rat! Gnaw rope! Rope won't whip butcher, butcher won't kill ox, ox won't drink water, water won't quench fire, fire won't burn stick, stick won't beat dog, dog won't bite pig, piggy won't jump over the stile, and I'll never get home tonight." But the rat would not.

She went a little further, and she met a cat, and she said, "Cat! Cat! Kill rat! Rat won't gnaw rope, rope won't whip butcher, butcher won't kill ox, ox won't drink water, water won't quench fire, fire won't burn stick, stick won't beat dog, dog won't bite pig, piggy won't jump over the stile, and I'll never get home tonight." And the cat said, "If you fetch me a saucer of milk, I will."

The woman brought the cat a saucer of milk, and as soon as the cat had lapped it up, the cat began to kill the rat, the rat began to gnaw the rope, the rope began to whip the butcher, the butcher began to kill the ox, the ox began to drink the

70

water, the water began to quench the fire, the fire began to burn the stick, the stick began to beat the dog, the dog began to bite the pig, the pig jumped over the stile, and the woman got home that night after all.

DIRECTIONS

Begin telling this story with the woman placed near the bottom center of the flannel board. Later, place the pig to her right and the stile to her left. Add some business of her pushing and pulling the pig if you wish. Though the text repeats "she went a little further," you can leave the woman just where she is until the end of the tale. Add each new character to the flannel board in a counter-clockwise circular pattern, ending with the cat and the bowl of milk just to the left of the woman. Remove the story figures one by one just as they begin to perform the tasks the woman has asked of them, and end with the pig taking a flying leap over the stile (pick him up and place him on the other side of it).

Participation

Young children love this story, and they enjoy being able to learn it. The flannel board figures help their memories. As you go through each recitation of who-won't-do-what, pause briefly before you mention each character's name: ". . . ox won't drink (pause) water, water won't quench (pause) fire. . . ." This gives the children a chance to say the word first, and your saying it is confirmation that they are right.

Follow-up

Leave the flannel board set up with all the figures on it, and let the children draw the story—it is really sort of a story-map—onto a piece of paper. They can use their drawings to tell the story themselves.

THE OLD WOMAN AND HER PIG

73

OX

STICK

ROPE

SAUCER

STILE

74

The Gunny Wolf

AN AFRO-AMERICAN TALE

A MAN and his little daughter lived alone in a cozy house in the forest. One morning the father had to go away, and he told the girl she must on no account go outside their yard, for that was the forest, and out there lived the wild animals.

The little girl played in the yard for a while. Then she spied some little blue and purple flowers growing smack at the edge of the forest, and she thought she could just tippy-toe over to get them and then tippy-toe back home, and none of the wild animals would see her.

So she tippy-toes over to where the flowers are growing, and she sings a little song: "Kum-kwa ki-mo, tray-bla, tray-bla."

Suddenly she hears a noise, and she looks up, and there is the great grey gunny wolf himself, and he says, "Little girl! You sing that good little, sweet little song again!"

So the little girl, she sings, "Kum-kwa ki-mo, tray-bla, tray-bla."

And the old gunny wolf he closes his eyes, and the little girl starts to tippy-toe away, pit-a-pat, pit-a-pat, pit-a-pat, pit-a-pat.

But just then she hears a noise behind her, and she stops, and it is the old gunny wolf, and he says, "Little girl, whyfore you move?"

The little girl answers, "My wolf, my dear, on what occasion should I move?"

"You sing that good little, sweet little song again," says the gunny wolf.

So she sings, "Kum-kwa ki-mo, tray-bla, tray-bla."

And the old gunny wolf he closes his eyes, and the little girl starts to tippy-toe away, pit-a-pat, pit-a-pat, pit-a-pat, pit-a-pat.

But she hears a noise behind her, and she stops, and the old gunny wolf growls—Grrrrr!—and he says, "Little girl, why-fore you move?"

The little girl answers, "My wolf, my dear, on what occasion should I move?"

"You sing that good little, sweet little song again," says the gunny wolf.

So she sings, "Kum-kwa ki-mo, tray-bla, tray-bla."

And the old gunny wolf he closes his eyes, and the little girl starts to tippy-toe away, pit-a-pat, pit-a-pat, pit-a-pat, pit-a-pat.

This time, the little girl tippy-toes all the way back to her cozy house and she latches the door behind her, and the old grey gunny wolf, he never does catch her.

Participation

Make up a simple tune for "Kum-kwa ki-mo, tray-bla, tray-bla" and teach the children to sing it with you.

Follow-up

This story makes a good two-player creative dramatics activity, which you can narrate. If everyone wants to participate at once, divide your group into pairs of little girls (or boys) and gunny wolves. Designate one side of the room as "home" and the other side of the room as "forest."

DIRECTIONS

Make a house in the upper left of the flannel board, about 6″ square (follow the directions in "Making Story Figures for the Flannel Board," pp. 5–6). Cut the gunny wolf from grey felt, and make cuts along the dotted lines between ears and head. These, and the weight of the felt, will allow his ears to flop down over his eyes when he falls asleep. Place the flowers in the lower right of the flannel board. The girl sings her lullaby, the wolf falls asleep (flip ear down over eye), and on each "pit-a-pat, pit-a-pat" she moves a few inches closer to her house. You may want to extend the story by merely repeating the sequence a few more times before the girl is safely inside her house.

FLOWERS

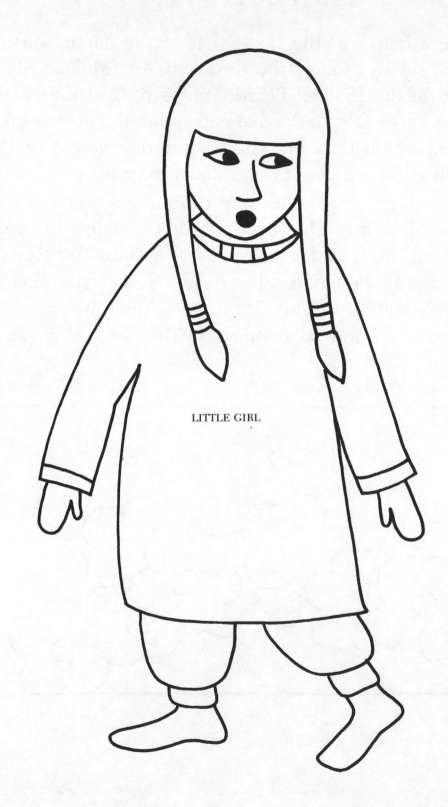

LITTLE GIRL

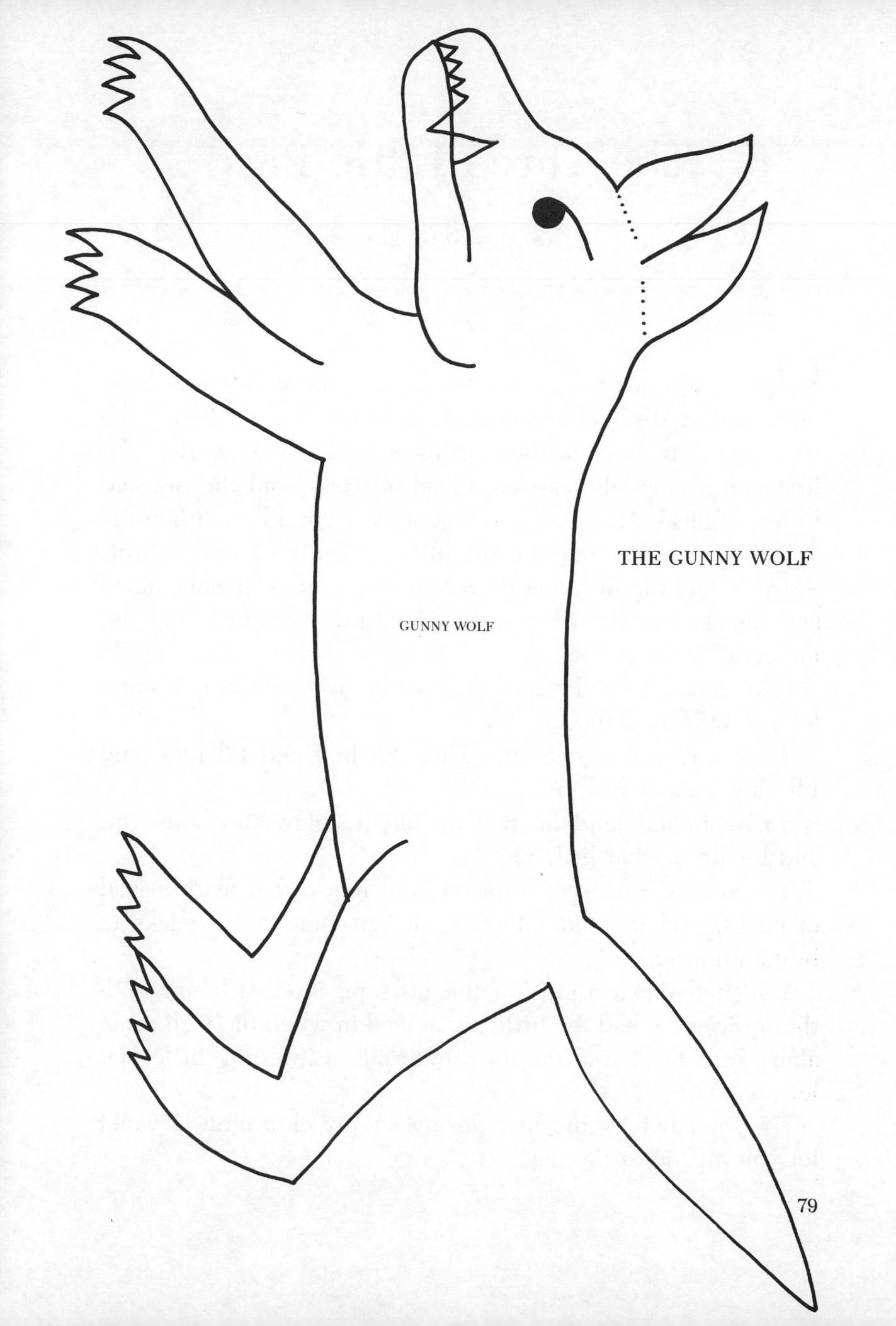

THE GUNNY WOLF

GUNNY WOLF

The Three Little Pigs

AN ENGLISH TALE

Once upon a time there was an old sow with three little pigs, and as she had not enough at home to keep them, she sent them out to seek their fortunes in the wide world. The first met a man who carried a load of straw, and the pig said to him, "Please, sir, give me that straw to build me a house."

Which the man did, and the little pig built a house with it. Scarcely had the little pig moved in when the wolf came along and knocked at the door and said, "Little pig, little pig, let me come in."

"No, no, not by the hair on my chinny chin chin, I won't let you in!" cried the pig.

Then the wolf answered, "Then I'll huff and I'll puff, and I'll blow your house in."

So he huffed, and he puffed, and he blew the house in, and he ate up that little pig.

The second little pig went out and met a man with a load of sticks, and he said, "Please, sir, give me those sticks to build a house."

Which the man did, and the little pig built a house with them. Scarcely had the little pig moved in when the wolf came along and knocked at the door and said, "Little pig, little pig, let me come in."

"No, no, not by the hair on my chinny chin chin, I won't let you in!" cried the pig.

Then the wolf answered, "Then I'll huff and I'll puff, and I'll blow your house in."

So he huffed, and he puffed, and he puffed, and he huffed, and he blew the house in, and he ate up the little pig.

The third little pig went out, and he met a man with a load of bricks, and the pig said, "Please, sir, give me those bricks to build a house with."

So the man gave him the bricks, and he built a house with them. No sooner had the pig moved in than the wolf came along, and knocked at the door, and said, "Little pig, little pig, let me come in."

"No, no, not by the hair on my chinny chin chin."

"Then I'll huff, and I'll puff, and I'll blow your house in."

Well, he huffed, and he puffed, and he huffed, and he puffed, and he puffed, and he huffed, but he could not get the house down. When he found he could not, he said to himself that he would climb up on the roof and go in through the chimney.

But the third little pig was watching him, and he built a fire in the fireplace, and put a big kettle of water on it. When the wolf slid down the chimney, he landed kerplunk in the water, and whether the pig ate him for dinner, or threw him out the door, I don't know.

Participation

Children will love to join in the refrains—"Little pig, little pig, let me come in!" and "Not by the hair of my chinny chin chin"—and to help with the wolf's huffing and puffing. When they know the story well, you can assign a speaking part to each of four children, and have them say the four characters' lines as you narrate and move the flannel board figures.

DIRECTIONS

Cut the houses of colored felt and the small bundles of sticks, straw, and bricks out of matching colors.

As you begin the story, the flannel board should be empty. There is no figure for the mother pig; the events on the flannel board begin when the first pig goes out and meets the man with the load of straw. When this pig builds a house, remove the bundle of straw from the flannel board and place the house over the pig so that the pig's face shows in the window. When the wolf blows the house away and eats the little pig, lift house and pig quickly off the flannel board. Likewise, lift the wolf off the board when he goes down the chimney of the house of the third pig.

The fact that these "disappeared" story characters are really in your hand or lap may distract some literal-minded children, so you will need to develop some of the magician's skill of directing their attention to the flannel board and away from your hand.

Many of our Disney-bred children object to the first two pigs being eaten. As an alternative, the two can run away from the wolf and appear at the third pig's door at the end of the story.

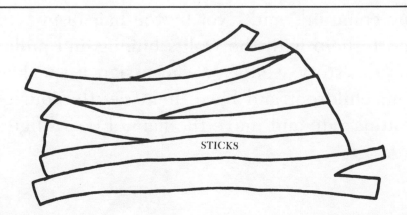

STICKS

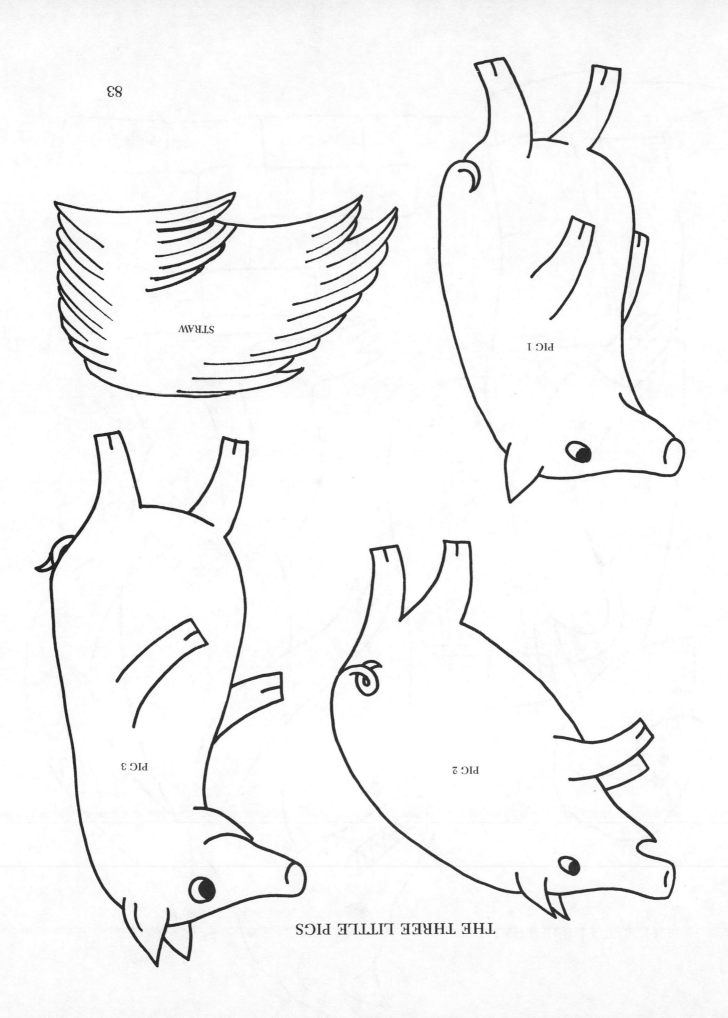

83

STRAW

PIG 1

PIG 3

PIG 2

THE THREE LITTLE PIGS

THE THREE LITTLE PIGS

WOLF

MAN

BRICKS

84

THE THREE LITTLE PIGS

CUT OUT

STICK HOUSE

CUT OUT

STRAW HOUSE

85

CUT OUT

BRICK HOUSE

The Little Red Hen

AN ENGLISH TALE

ONCE, A cat, a dog, a mouse, and a little red hen all lived together in a little house. The cat, the dog, and the mouse did nothing from morning until night, so the little red hen cleaned and cooked and did all the housework.

Early one morning, the little red hen was sweeping in the yard when she found a little tiny grain of wheat.

"Who will help me plant this wheat?" she asked.

"Not I!" said the cat.

"Not I!" said the dog.

"Not I!" said the mouse.

"Then I will," said the little red hen, and she did. She planted the tiny grain of wheat, and she watered it, and she tended it, and it grew ripe.

"Who will help me harvest the wheat?" asked the little red hen.

"Not I!" said the cat.

"Not I!" said the dog.

"Not I!" said the mouse.

"Then I will," said the little red hen, and she did. And when the grain was cut and threshed, she asked, "Who will help me take this wheat to the miller's to be ground into flour?"

"Not I!" said the cat.

"Not I!" said the dog.

"Not I!" said the mouse.

"Then I will," said the little red hen, and she did. When

she had returned from the miller's with the flour, the hen asked, "Who will help me bake a cake?"

"Not I!" said the cat.

"Not I!" said the dog.

"Not I!" said the mouse.

"Then I will," said the little red hen, and she did. She mixed the flour with milk and eggs and honey, and put the batter into the oven to bake. Soon the wonderful smell of cake filled the little house.

"Who will help me eat this cake?" asked the little red hen.

"I will!" said the cat.

"I will!" said the dog.

"I will!" said the mouse.

But the little red hen said "No! All by myself I planted the wheat, I watered it and tended it, and all by myself I harvested it. All by myself I took it to the miller's to be ground into flour, and all by myself I mixed and baked the cake, and ALL BY MYSELF I am going to eat it!"

And she did!

Participation

After introducing the story, have the group join in saying "Not I!" and "I will!" for the cat, the dog, and the mouse. Help them practice using a different kind of voice (gruff, whining, squeaky) for each different animal.

Follow-up

As a follow-up activity, have the children mime the actions and say the words of the little red hen as you narrate the story. Each child can stand and perform the hen's actions in her own place and in her own way. As a treat, follow this activity with biscuits and honey for all the good workers.

DIRECTIONS

Make a house toward the right side of the flannel board, about 8″ square (follow the directions in "Making Story Figures for the Flannel Board," pp. 5–6). Place the stove in the house before you begin to tell the story. As you name the animals—dog, cat, and mouse—place them across the bottom of the flannel board beneath the house, and place the hen to the left of the house.

The hen can remain stationary until she goes into the house with the flour to make the cake. Use the little props—wheat, flour, cake—like this:

(1) Hen finds wheat—wheat is imaginary;
(2) Hen plants wheat—place watering can on her wing;
(3) Wheat grows—take away watering can and place wheat stalk on the ground;
(4) Hen cuts wheat—place wheat stalk on her wing;
(5) Hen gets flour—remove wheat stalk and put flour sack on her wing;
(6) Hen bakes cake—put her inside house and place cake in oven;
(7) Hen serves cake—put cake on her wing;
(8) Hen eats cake—remove cake from flannel board.

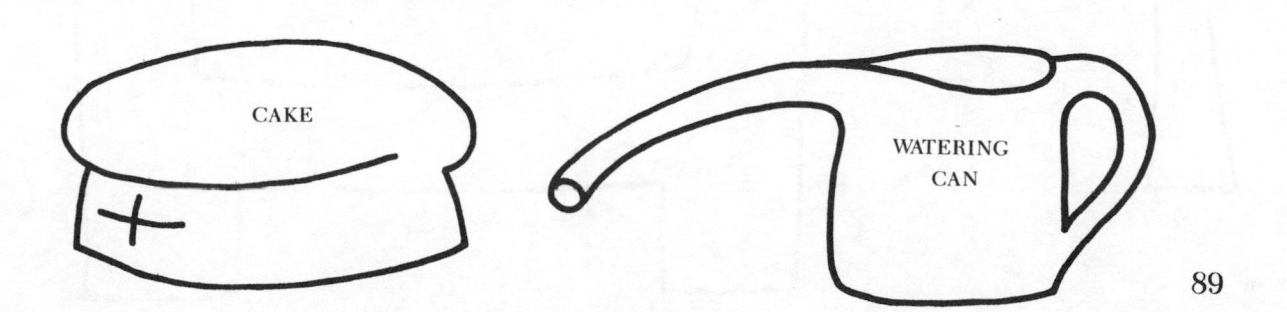

CAKE

WATERING CAN

89

ARCADIA PUBLIC LIBRARY
ARCADIA, WISCONSIN 54612

FLOUR

THE LITTLE RED HEN

LITTLE RED HEN

WHEAT

OVEN

CAT

MOUSE

DOG

I Got Me a Cat

AN AMERICAN FOLK SONG

I got me a cat, my cat pleased me,

I fed my cat un - der yon - der tree,

and the (*) said (**),

and the cat said fid - dle - I - fee!

Participation

Keep the song going as long as everyone's memory for the long string of animals and noises holds out (the figures on the flannel board, placed in order, will help). The children can place their own animals on the flannel board as the song progresses.

92

DIRECTIONS

Begin the song with the tree at the center of the flannel board and the cat to one side. For the first verse, use bars 1, 2, 3, 4, 6, and 7. In subsequent verses, add other animals' names (*) and the noises they make (**), substituting the name of each new animal for "cat" in the first three bars—along the line of "Old MacDonald Had a Farm." Note that although the cat says "fiddle-I-fee," other animals' noises can be more realistic. For the other animals you may either take patterns from the other stories in this book or have the children draw and cut their own animals on felt or interfacing.

CAT

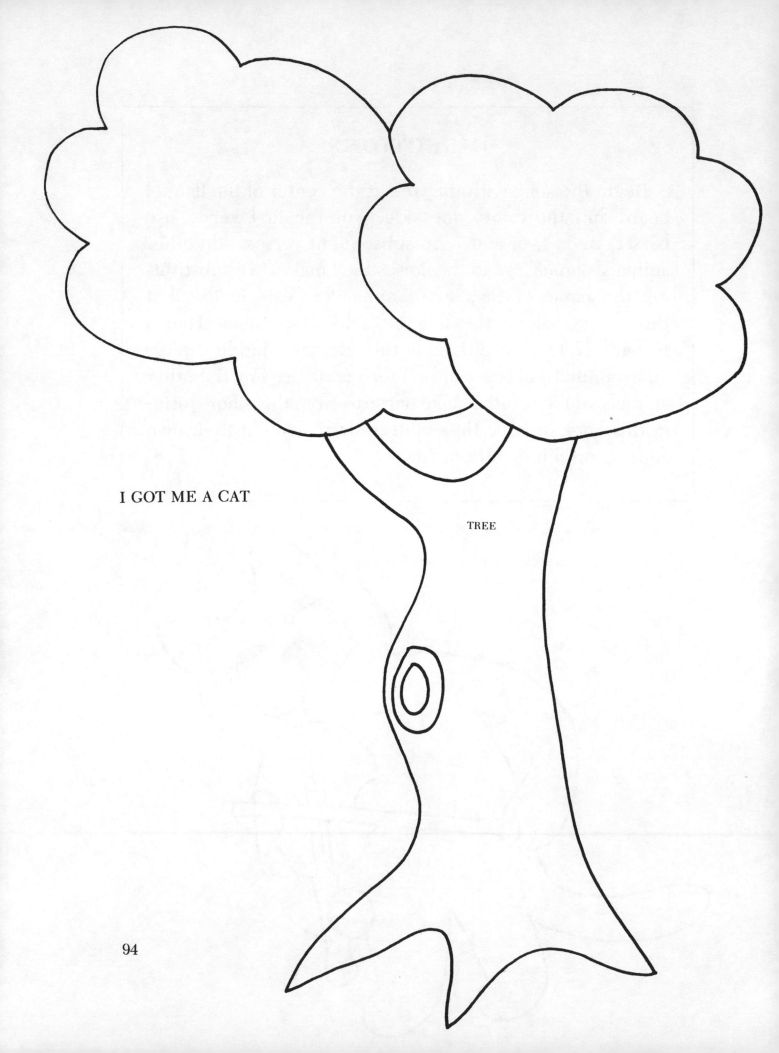

I GOT ME A CAT

TREE

94

Little Cockroach Martina

On a bright and sunny morning, little cockroach Martina found a gold coin in her yard. She picked it up. "What shall I buy with this?" she asked. "If I buy bread, I will just eat it all up and it will be gone. If I buy cheese, or rice, or candy, I will run out of those, too."

After much thinking and deciding, Martina bought herself a fancy tin of powder, and she powdered her face, put on her best dress, and stood on the patio of her little house.

Along came Señor Perro, the dog.

"Buenos días, Señorita Martina," he said. "I was wondering . . . would you marry me?"

"If I marry you, Señor Perro, how will you speak to me in the evening?" asked Martina.

"I will speak to you like this: Ruff! Ruff! Ruff, ruff, ruff!"

"Oh dear!" cried Martina. "You would frighten me with all your barking. No, Señor Perro, I will not marry you."

Señor Perro went away sadly, his tail between his legs.

Along came Señor Gato, the cat.

"Buenos días, Señorita Martina," he said. "Tell me, will you marry me?"

"If I marry you, Señor Gato, how will you speak to me in the evening?" asked Martina.

"Me-owwww! Me-owwww! Me-owwww!" said the cat. "That is how I will speak to you."

"Ouch! Your voice hurts my ears, Señor Gato," said Martina. "I cannot marry you."

Señor Gato went away sadly, with his nose nearly touching the ground.

Along came Señor Sapo, the toad.

"Buenos días, Señorita Martina," said the toad. "I would like to ask you, please, will you marry me?"

"If I marry you, Señor Sapo, how will you speak to me in the evening?" asked Martina.

"I will speak to you like this: Bo-roooom! Bo-roooom! Bo-rooom!" replied the toad.

"Oh, no!" cried Martina. "Your voice is very unpleasant! I will not marry you."

Señor Sapo hopped away with big tears in his eyes.

Then, along came Señor Perez, the mouse.

"Buenos días, Señorita Martina," said the mouse. "I have been wanting to ask you a certain question, beautiful señorita . . . will you marry me?"

"If I marry you, Señor Perez, how will you speak to me in the evening?" asked Martina.

"Señorita, I will speak to you like this: Cheery-cheery-chee! Cheery-cheery-chee! Cheery-cheery-chee!"

"Oh, how beautiful your voice is!" cried Martina. "Yes, Señor Perez, yes! I will marry you."

Perez and Martina were married in a grand wedding. Señor Sapo, Señor Gato, and Señor Perro all came and gave them presents.

Every day, Martina the cockroach powders her face, and every day, Perez the mouse loves her more than the day before.

Participation

Have different children help with the sounds that the dog, cat, toad, and Perez make for Martina. You may even wish to add other animals and sounds to make the story longer and to use more Spanish words.

DIRECTIONS

In this story, Martina the cockroach is like a paper doll, changing dresses for evening and wedding. Make her patio by placing the plant at the right of the flannel board and the little fence about 7″ to the left of it. She will stand between these two as she receives her suitors. For her wedding, move Martina so that she is facing Perez, touching hands, and put her wedding dress on her.

Follow-up

Make simple stick puppets from the patterns and color them on both sides. Make three Martina puppets: one plain, one in fancy evening dress, and one in her wedding dress. Have an orchestra of kazoos and tambourines play a Latin song after the wedding, so that all of the puppets can dance.

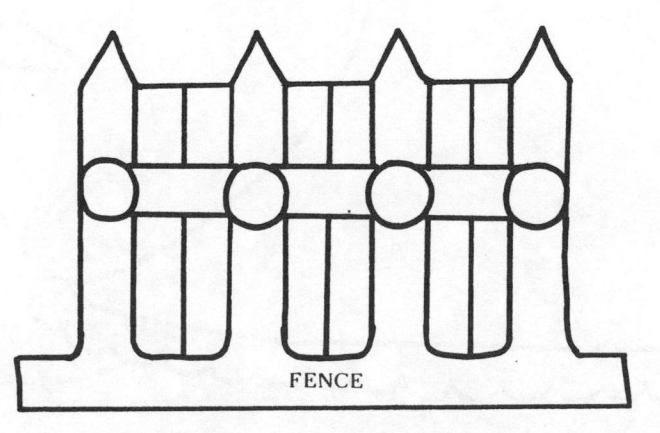

FENCE

LITTLE COCKROACH MARTINA

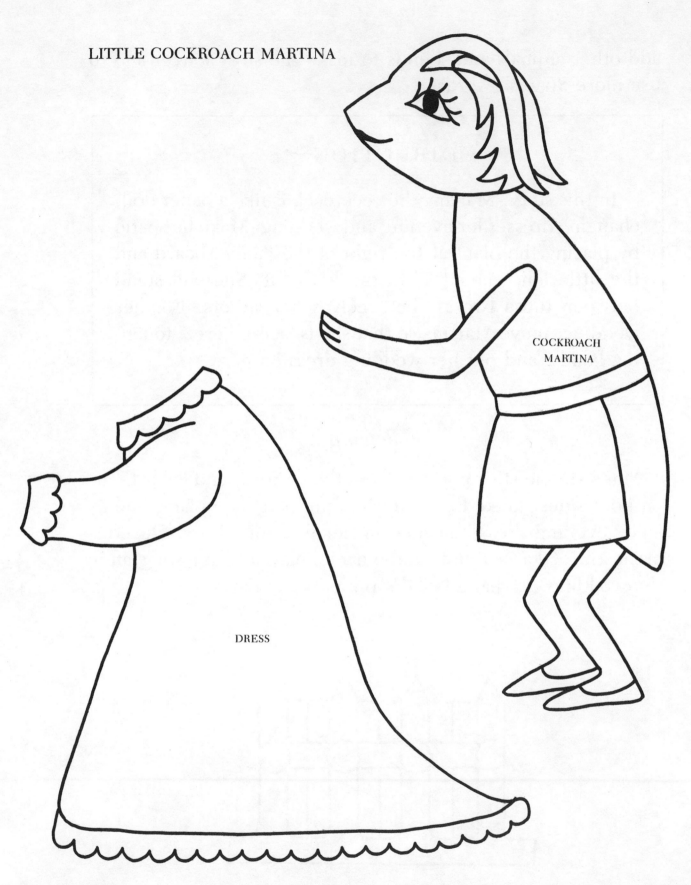

COCKROACH
MARTINA

DRESS

66

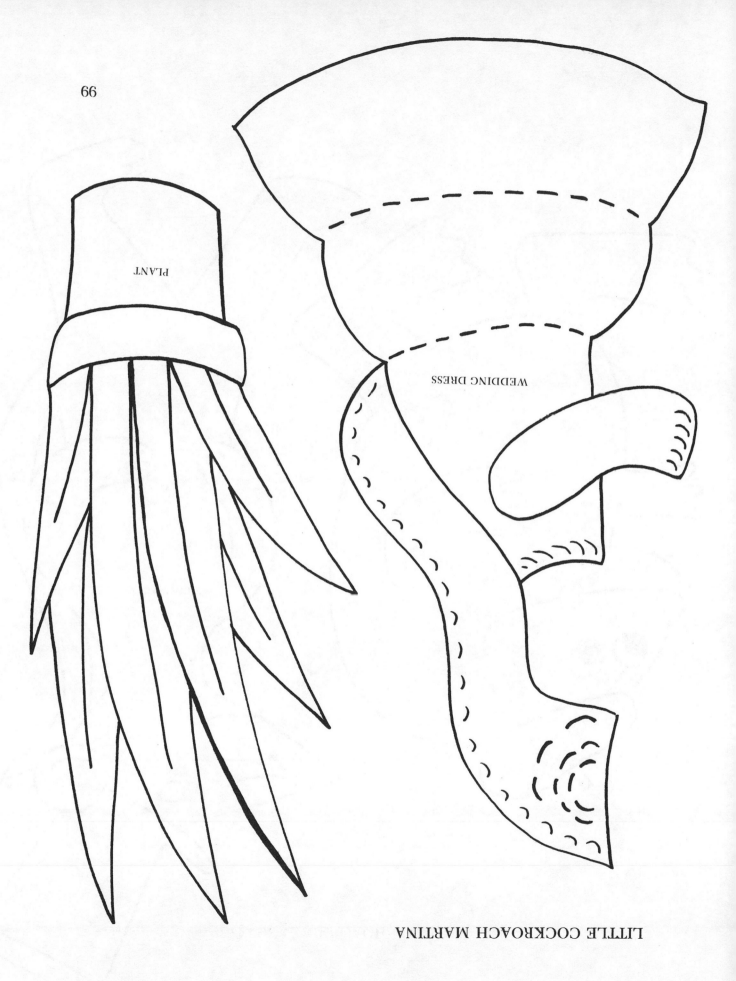

PLANT

WEDDING DRESS

LITTLE COCKROACH MARTINA

SEÑOR PEREZ

SEÑOR SAPO

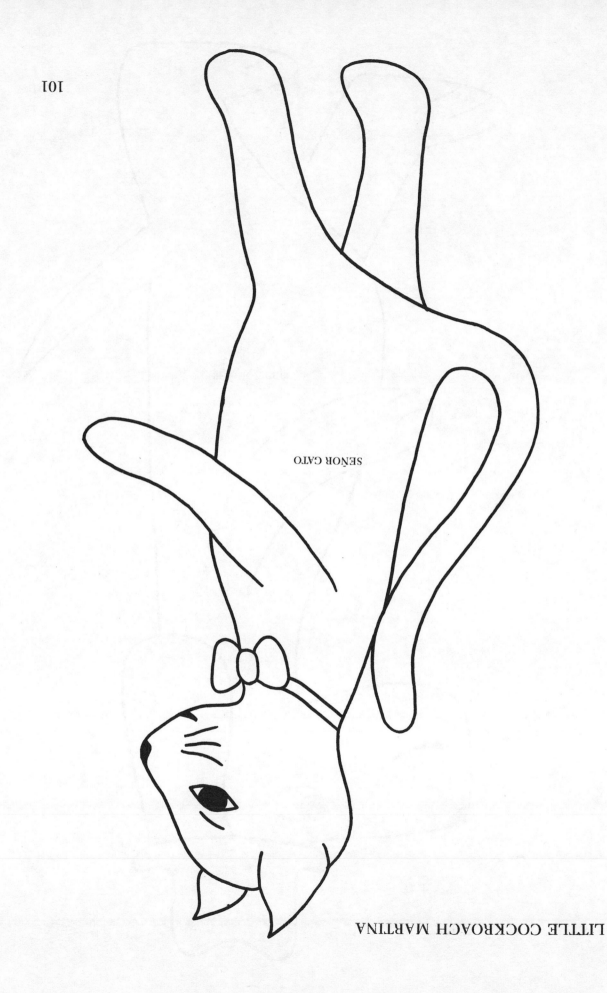

SEÑOR GATO

LITTLE COCKROACH MARTINA

SEÑOR PERRO

102

Part II

FOR CHILDREN
FIVE TO EIGHT YEARS OLD

The Fearsome Beast

AN AFRICAN (MASAI) TALE

ONE MORNING, a little caterpillar crawled into the hollow log that was Rabbit's house. Rabbit was away, and when he returned he saw the marks of Caterpillar's feet on the ground and he cried out, "Who is in my house?"

Caterpillar answered in a loud voice (and the hollow log made it even louder), "I am a great warrior, son of the long one! I crush the rhinoceros to the earth, and I make dust of the elephant. I am invincible!"

Rabbit was afraid, and he said to himself, "What can a small animal like myself do against a warrior who tramples the elephant into dust?" So Rabbit called on Leopard to come and help him.

Leopard came, and growled fiercely, and said, "Who is in the house of my friend Rabbit?"

Caterpillar answered, "I am a great warrior, son of the long one! I crush the rhinoceros to the earth, and I make dust of the elephant. I am invincible!"

Leopard backed off, saying, "If he crushes the elephant and the rhinoceros, he will do the same to me!" And Leopard went away.

Next, Rabbit called on Rhinoceros, but when Rhinoceros heard what Caterpillar had to say, he cried, "What? He can crush me to earth? I'd better leave here fast!"

Rabbit then tried Elephant, asking him to please rid his house of this monster. But when Elephant heard the caterpillar's boast, he told Rabbit that he had no desire to be trampled underfoot like dust, and stomped away.

Now, Frog had been sitting under a leaf nearby, watching and listening to everything that had happened. Frog went up to Rabbit's door and asked who was inside.

Caterpillar replied, "I am a great warrior, son of the long one! I crush the rhinoceros to earth, and I make dust of the elephant. I am invincible!"

Frog went right up to the hollow log and said in a great, loud voice of his own, "Borooommm! Borooommm! I am the mighty leaper! The ground splits where I sit, and the Creator has made me green, slimy, and vile!"

When Caterpillar heard this, he trembled and said, "But I am only a caterpillar! Please, don't hurt me!"

Rabbit and Frog dragged Caterpillar out of the house, and they laughed and laughed at all the trouble he had caused everyone.

DIRECTIONS

Cut the log of brown felt and place it to the right hand side of the flannel board as the story begins. When Caterpillar climbs inside the hollow log, simply lift the log and put him under it. Place the rabbit to the left of the log and below it, so that the other animals can be placed just above him.

Participation

Have the children learn Caterpillar's chant, "I am the great warrior . . . ," and repeat it together during the story.

CATERPILLAR

FROG

RABBIT

HOLLOW LOG

LEOPARD

THE FEARSOME BEAST

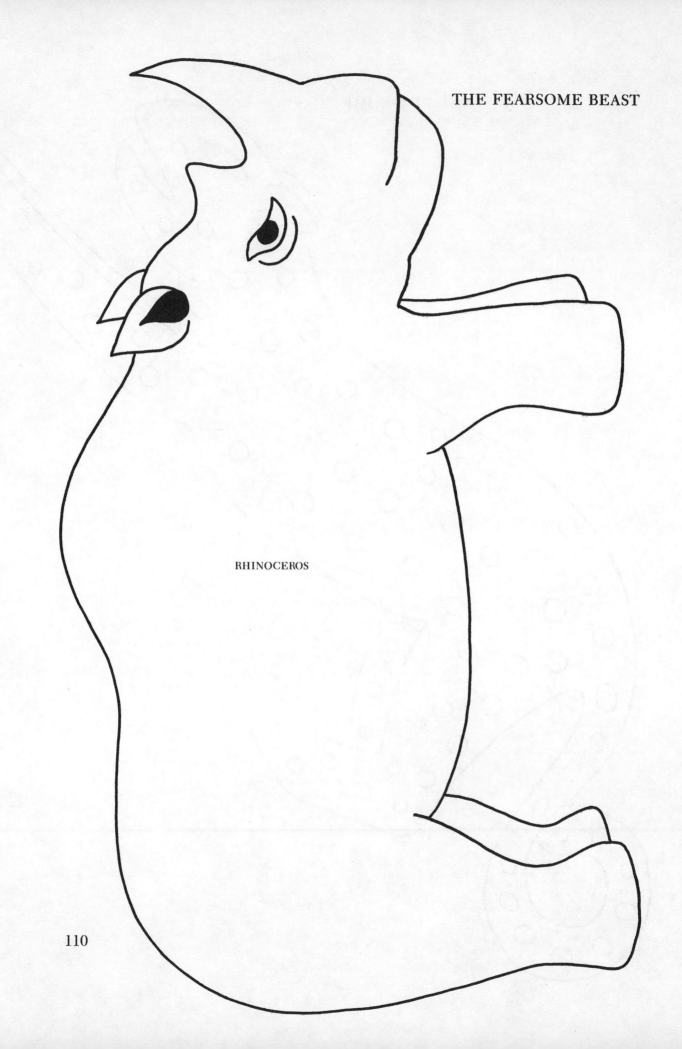

RHINOCEROS

110

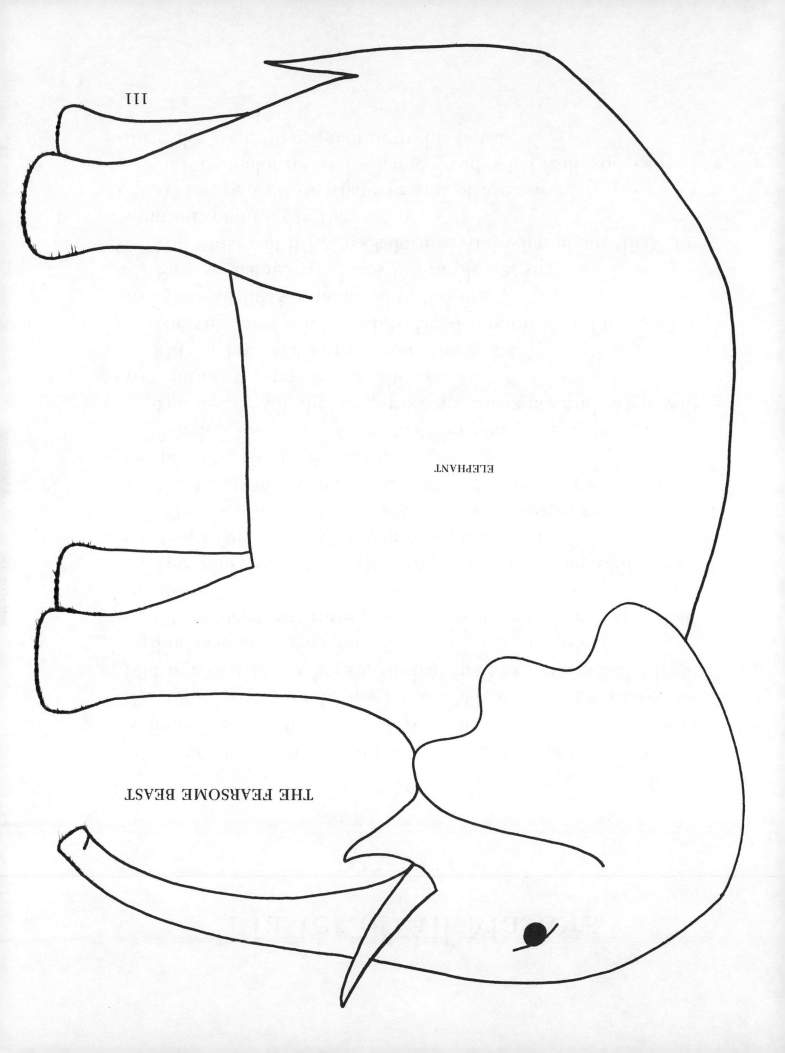

III

ELEPHANT

THE FEARSOME BEAST

Master of All Masters

AN ENGLISH TALE

A GIRL once went to the fair to hire herself out as a servant. A funny old gentleman said yes, she would do, and would she come with him to his house. When they got there, he told her that in *his* house, he had his own names for things.

"For instance, what would you call me?" he asked.

"Oh, master, or mister, or whatever you please, sir!" said the girl.

"You must call me master of all masters," he said. "And what will you call this?"—pointing to the bed.

"Why, bed, or couch, or whatever you please, sir."

"No, this is my barnacle. And what do you call these?" asked he, pointing to his pantaloons.

"Britches, or trousers, or whatever you please, sir."

"You must call them squibs and crackers! And what will you call her?"—pointing to the cat.

"Cat, or kit, or whatever you please, sir."

"No, you must call her white-faced simminy. And now, what will you call this?"—pointing to the fire.

"Fire, or flame, or whatever you please, sir."

"You must call it hot cockalorum! And what about this?" he went on, pointing to the water.

"Water, or wet, or whatever you please, sir."

"No! Pondalorum is its name. And what will you call all this?" he continued, pointing to his house.

"House, or cottage, or whatever you please, sir."

"You must call it high topper mountain."*

That very night, the servant woke her master up in a fright and cried, "Master of all masters, master of all masters, get out of your barnacle and put on your squibs and crackers, for white-faced simminy has got a spark of hot cockalorum on her tail, and unless you get some pondalorum, high topper mountain will be all on hot cockalorum!"

That's all!

DIRECTIONS

Begin the story with the girl on the flannel board, then add the old man. When they go to his house, add the peaked roof above them to indicate this. Then, add each new item as the old man talks about it. At *, put the man into the bed and slowly move the flame to the cat's tail.

Participation

Children will love learning all the silly names for things. As you repeat the story for them, call on the children to give the old man's name for each thing at the appropriate time in the story.

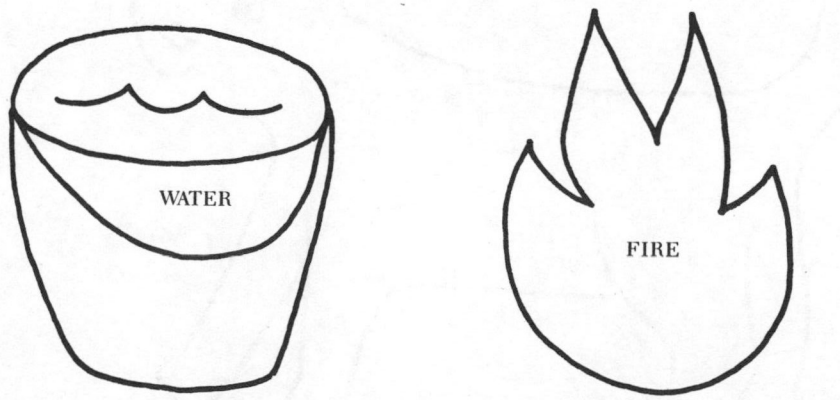

WATER

FIRE

OLD GENTLEMAN

GIRL

MASTER OF ALL MASTERS

CAT

114

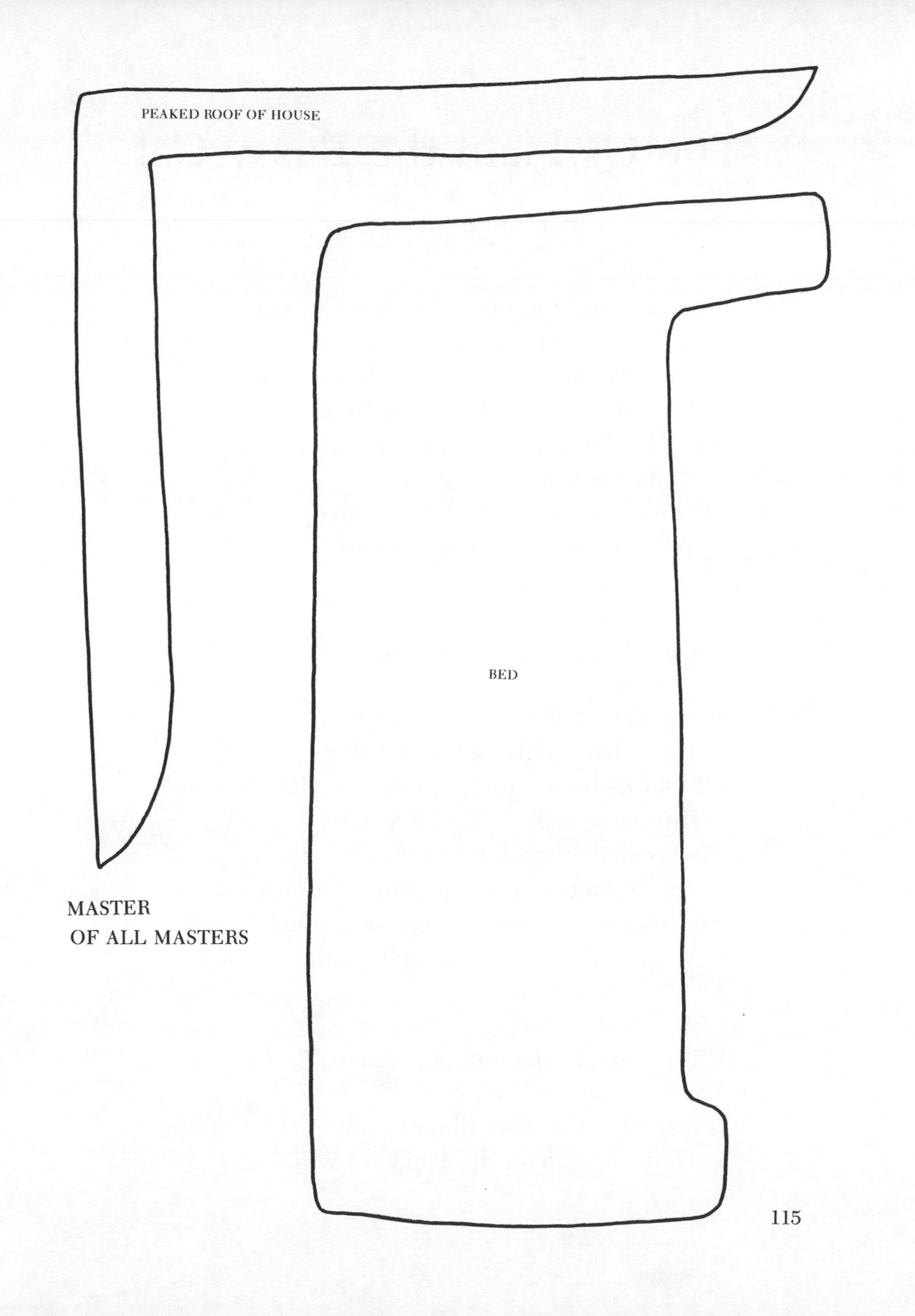

PEAKED ROOF OF HOUSE

BED

MASTER
OF ALL MASTERS

115

The Owl and the Pussy-Cat

A POEM BY EDWARD LEAR

The Owl and the Pussy-Cat went to sea
 In a beautiful pea-green boat:
They took some honey, and plenty of money
 Wrapped up in a five-pound note.
The Owl looked up to the stars above,
 And sang to a small guitar,
"O lovely Pussy, O Pussy, my love,
 What a beautiful Pussy you are,
   You are,
   You are!
What a beautiful Pussy you are!"

Pussy said to the Owl, "You elegant fowl,
 How charmingly sweet you sing!
Oh! let us be married; too long we have tarried!
 But what shall we do for a ring?"
They sailed away, for a year and a day,
 To the land where the bong-tree grows;
And there in a wood a Piggy-wig stood,
 With a ring at the end of his nose,
   His nose,
   His nose,
With a ring at the end of his nose.

"Dear Pig, are you willing to sell for one shilling
 Your ring?" Said the Piggy, "I will."

So they took it away, and were married next day
    By the turkey who lives on the hill.
They dined on mince and slices of quince,
    Which they ate with a runcible spoon;
And hand in hand, on the edge of the sand,
    They danced by the light of the moon
        The moon,
        The moon,
They danced by the light of the moon.

DIRECTIONS

Cut the story characters from interfacing or felt, and the boat and island from felt. This story is basically a tableau, with little moving of the story figures. Using figures on a flannel board is a lovely excuse for learning and telling a marvelously absurd poem, and the children can and should learn it too.

Set the island to the right, with Piggy to the left of the bong tree and the turkey to the right. Place the moon above and the boat to the left with Owl and Pussy-Cat in it. Move the boat, and Owl and Pussy-Cat, as the story dictates. The ring on Piggy's nose is a separate piece, and for fun you can place it around the cat's tail during the wedding.

Follow-up

After several tellings of the poem, put the flannel board and figures away and have the children draw a picture of the poem, trying to include everything mentioned in it. See how many are able to remember every detail.

PUSSY-CAT

OWL

119

PIGGY

THE OWL AND THE PUSSY-CAT

TURKEY

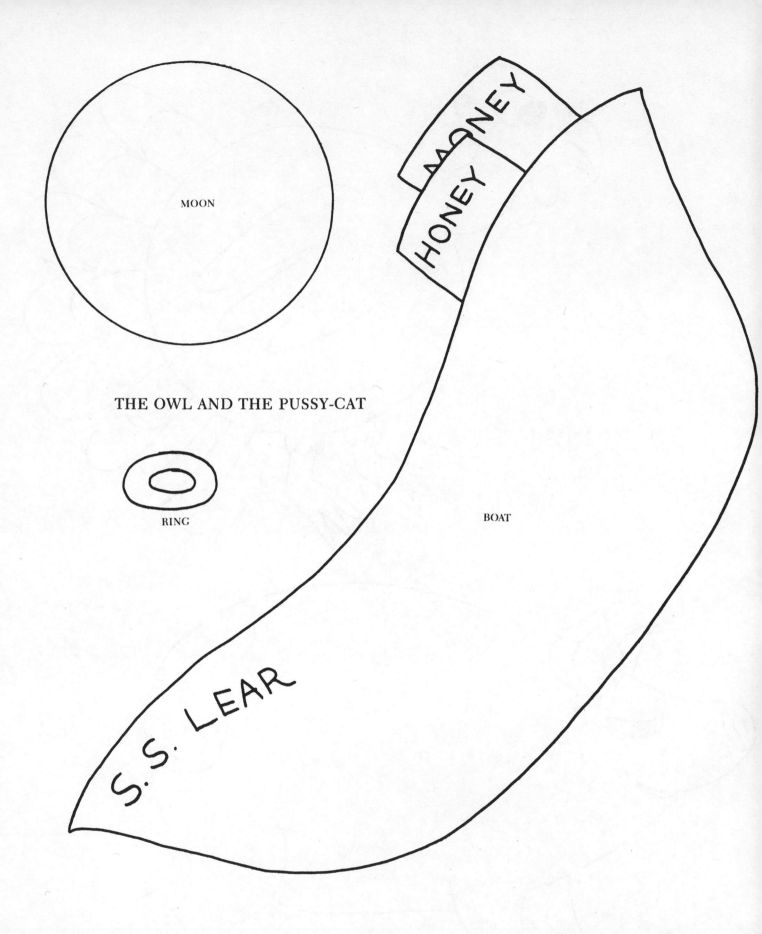

MOON

THE OWL AND THE PUSSY-CAT

RING

MONEY

HONEY

BOAT

S.S. LEAR

120

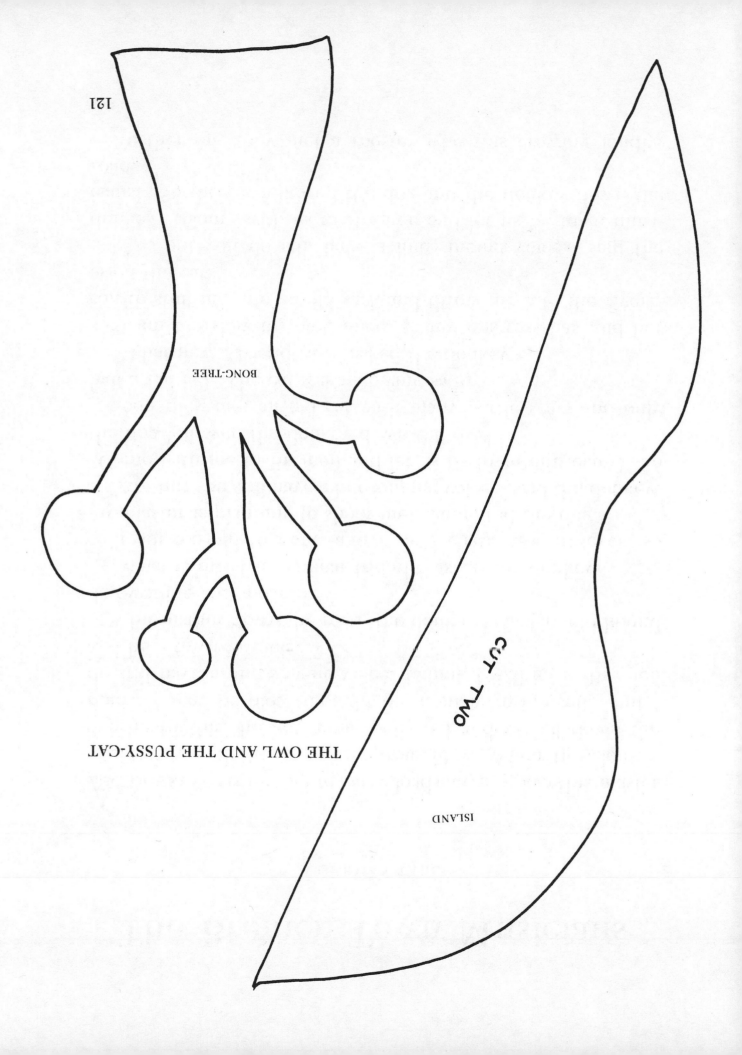

121

BONG-TREE

CUT TWO

THE OWL AND THE PUSSY-CAT

ISLAND

The Bremen Town Musicians

A GERMAN TALE

A DONKEY was too old to carry loads anymore, so his master decided to sell the animal for slaughter. When the donkey overheard this, he left home pell-mell and set off down the road. "I may be old," thought the donkey to himself, "but I do still have a fine singing voice. I think I will go to Bremen and be a town musician."

A bit further down the road, the donkey heard an old hound dog wailing and moaning.

"What is the matter, dear friend?" asked the donkey.

"I am too old to hunt, and I can't chase away thieves, so my master is planning to shoot me!" lamented the dog.

"Ah, but you still have a fine singing voice," said the donkey. "Come with me to Bremen and let us be town musicians!" So the dog followed the donkey down the road.

Soon they met an old cat with many battle scars and only half a tail left. The cat was meowing sadly.

"What news, friend cat?" asked the donkey.

"I am too slow to catch mice, so my mistress has told her son to stuff me into an old sack and throw me into the river!" cried the cat.

"Ah, but you do still have a fine singing voice," said the donkey. "Come with us to Bremen and let us be town musicians!" So the cat followed the dog and the donkey down the road.

Further on, they met a rooster who was crowing loudly.

"Why so noisy, friend rooster?" asked the donkey. "The sun rose many hours ago."

"My mistress has told the cook to chop off my head and serve me for dinner," said the rooster. "So I am crowing while I still have a beak to crow with!"

"Why go into the soup pot, when you can come with us to Bremen and be a town musician?" asked the donkey. No sooner said than done: the rooster followed the donkey, dog, and cat down the road.

As night fell, the animals began to think about lodgings, and in the distance they saw the lights of a house. The donkey walked up under the window, the dog jumped onto the donkey's back, the cat climbed onto the dog's back, and the rooster flapped up to the cat's back and looked into the house. This is what he saw: four robbers were sitting around a table that was heaped with all sorts of food and drink, and the robbers were counting gold coins into huge sacks!

The rooster described this astonishing scene to the other animals. "Let us sing a song for them," suggested the donkey. "Perhaps they will give us food and lodging."

All four animals opened their mouths and began to sing loud and hard. At the sound of all that braying, howling, yowling, and crowing, the frightened robbers ran away as fast as their legs could carry them.

The animals went into the house and had a good meal. Then, each settled down for the night: the donkey by the door, the dog under the table, the cat in the hearth, and the rooster on the table edge.

Meanwhile, the robbers began to feel foolish at being so afraid of a mere noise, so they sent one of their band back to the house to investigate. Warily the robber entered the house. He saw the cat's two eyes glowing in the hearth, and, mistaking them for two glowing embers of the fire, he tried to light a match on them. The cat reached out and clawed his face! The dog lurched from under the table and bit the man's leg, the rooster crowed "cock-a-doodle-doo," and the donkey kicked that robber out the door!

The robber ran back to his companions and reported what he had found: "There is a witch by the fireplace who tried to scratch my eyes out! Then a monster stabbed my leg with a knife, a ghost yelled "cut-the-fool-in-two! . . ." and a giant with a club hit me on my way out the door!"

The robbers never went back to that house. As for our four animal friends, why, they had enough gold to keep them in comfort the rest of their lives. But the poor, unfortunate people of Bremen never had the pleasure of listening to them sing.

DIRECTIONS

Color the animals on both sides. Begin the story with the donkey placed to the right of the center of the flannel board, facing right. He meets the other animals head to head, then they fall into line behind him. When the animals look into the robbers' window, they do so at the far right hand edge of the board (the window is imaginary).

In the second scene of the story, the interior of the house is represented by the table. Set up the sleeping animals so that there is just room for the robber to the right of the table, between the cat, dog, and donkey, who are all facing him.

When the robber is reporting back to the other robbers at the end of the story, hold him in your hand so the children can still see him while you talk about him.

Follow-up

Divide the group into cats, dogs, roosters, and donkeys. Rehearse and give a (short!) concert by your own Bremen Town Musicians.

This is also a good story to act out in creative dramatics, as there is much room for action and improvised dialogue.

ROBBER

ROOSTER

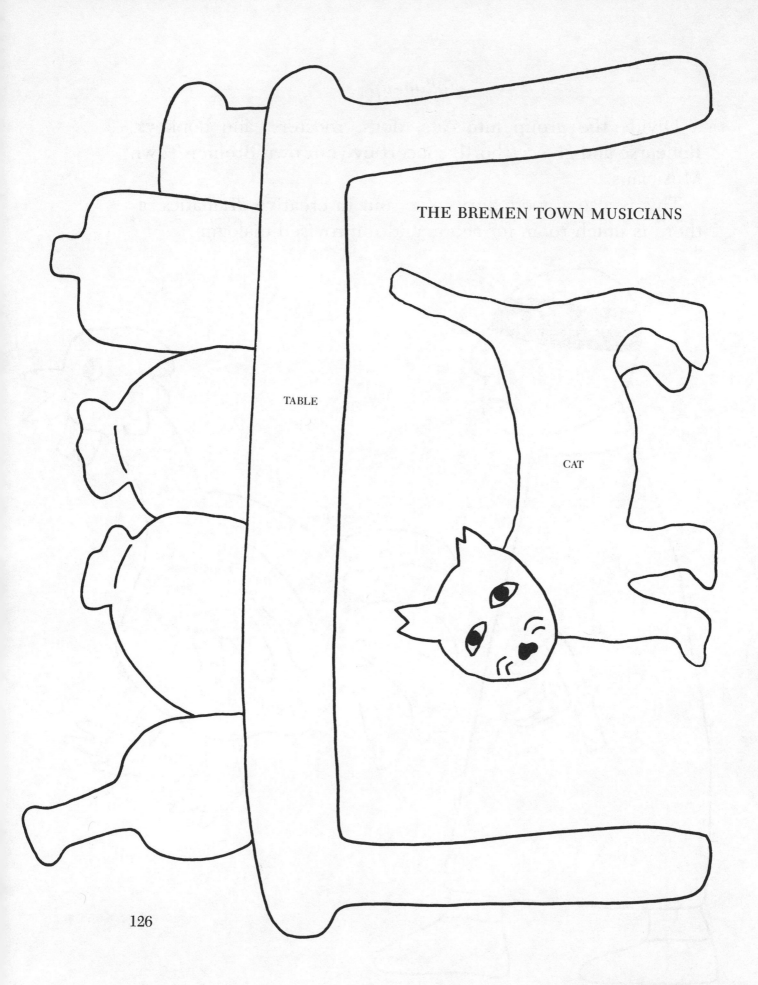

THE BREMEN TOWN MUSICIANS

TABLE

CAT

DONKEY

DOG

127

The Rat's Daughter

A JAPANESE TALE

THE RAT knew that his daughter was the most beautiful creature in the world. So, when the handsome young rat next door asked the rat for his daughter's hand in marriage, the rat said, "No, no, never! My beautiful daughter shall only marry the strongest one in the world."

And so the rat traveled to the place where the sun lives. "O mighty one!" said the rat. "I am looking for a husband for my daughter. She is so beautiful that she can only marry the strongest one in the world."

"You can't mean me," said the sun, "for there is one who is far stronger than I."

"Who could that be?" asked the rat. He could not imagine anyone stronger than the sun.

"The cloud," replied the sun. "The cloud covers my face and keeps my warmth from reaching the earth. The one you are looking for must be the cloud."

Then the rat traveled to see the cloud. "Greetings, great one!" said the rat. "I am searching for a husband for my daughter, who is the most beautiful rat in the world. This husband must be the most powerful one of all."

"You couldn't possibly mean me," laughed the cloud, "for the smallest puff of wind sends me sailing across the sky. You must be looking for the wind."

The rat hurried off to the home of the wind. When he got there, he said, "Mighty Wind, I am looking for a suitable hus-

128

band for my daughter, the loveliest rat in the world. This husband must, like yourself, be the strongest of all."

"Me?" demanded the wind. "Oh, no, there is one who is far, far stronger than I."

"Who is that?" asked the rat. He was tired from all his traveling.

"It is the stone wall. The stone wall stops me dead in my tracks. The one you seek has to be the stone wall."

The rat traveled until he saw a high stone wall. "Oh, admirable Stone Wall!" the rat said. "I am looking for a suitable husband for my daughter, the world's loveliest rat. This husband, like yourself, must be the strongest one of all."

"Then it is not me that you seek," replied the stone wall, "for a creature far more powerful than I is right now, this very minute, destroying me, gnawing and chewing away at my very foundations . . . the rat is far stronger than I."

"Thank you," said the rat. He returned home to announce the marriage of his lovely daughter to the handsome young rat next door, who was, it seemed, the strongest creature of all. And it was him that his daughter had wanted to marry all along.

Follow-up

"The Rat's Daughter" is fun to act out as a creative drama with masks, or as a simple stick puppet play. Use the patterns to make simple stick puppets of heavy paper, and color them on both sides. Sticks for the puppets can be pencils, chopsticks, or bamboo skewers. Use the flannel board as a puppet stage, or make one from a cardboard box.

DIRECTIONS

The rat, in his travels, never leaves his spot on the flannel board. Begin the story with him slightly to the left of center of the board. Place his daughter facing him and (when his time comes) the suitor behind her. These two are both removed when the rat begins his travels. Each of the other characters in turn—the sun, cloud, wind, and wall—is placed to the right of the rat (the sun, cloud, and wind higher up, of course). Finally, return to the early scene of the rat, his daughter, and her suitor.

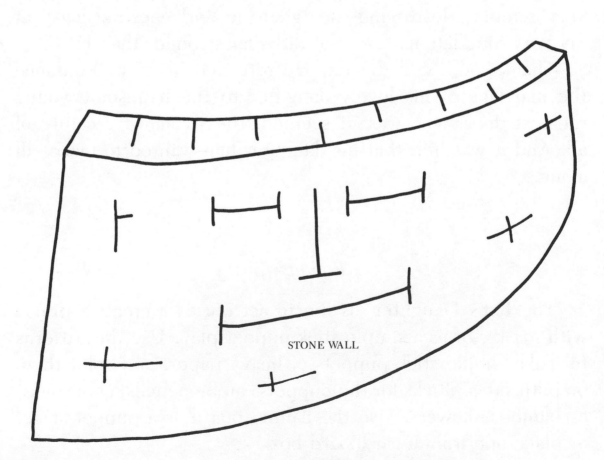

STONE WALL

HANDSOME RAT

RAT

THE RAT'S DAUGHTER

WIND

THE RAT'S DAUGHTER

DAUGHTER

CLOUD

THE RAT'S DAUGHTER

SUN

The Strange Visitor

AN ENGLISH POEM

A woman was sitting at her reel one night;
  And still she sat, and still she reeled, and still she wished
    for company.

In came a pair of broad broad feet, and sat down at the
    fireside;
  And still she sat, and still she reeled, and still she wished
    for company.

In came a pair of small small legs, and sat down on the broad
    broad feet;
  And still she sat, and still she reeled, and still she wished
    for company.

In came a pair of thick thick knees, and sat down on the
    small small legs;
  And still she sat, and still she reeled, and still she wished
    for company.

In came a pair of thin thin thighs, and sat down on the thick
    thick knees;
  And still she sat, and still she reeled, and still she wished
    for company.

In came a pair of huge huge hips, and sat down on the thin
    thin thighs;

134

And still she sat, and still she reeled, and still she wished
for company.

In came a wee wee waist, and sat down on the huge huge
hips;
And still she sat, and still she reeled, and still she wished
for company.

In came a pair of broad broad shoulders, and sat down on the
wee wee waist;
And still she sat, and still she reeled, and still she wished
for company.

In came a pair of small small arms, and sat down on the
broad broad shoulders;
And still she sat, and still she reeled, and still she wished
for company.

In came a pair of huge huge hands, and sat down on the
small small arms;
And still she sat, and still she reeled, and still she wished
for company.

In came a small small neck, and sat down on the broad broad
shoulders;
And still she sat, and still she reeled, and still she wished
for company.

In came a huge huge head, and sat down on the small small
neck.

"How did you get such broad broad feet?" asked the woman.
(*gruffly*)   "Much tramping, much tramping."

"How did you get such small small legs?"
(*whiningly*) "Aih-h-h!—late—and *weee-e-e*—moul."

"How did you get such thick thick knees?"
(*piously*) "Much praying, much praying."

"How did you get such thin thin thighs?"
(*whiningly*) "Aih-h-h!—late—and *weee-e-e*—moul."

"How did you get such big big hips?"
(*gruffly*) "Much sitting, much sitting."

"How did you get such a wee wee waist?"
(*whiningly*) "Aih-h-h!—late—and *weee-e-e*—moul."

"How did you get such broad, broad shoulders?"
(*gruffly*) "With carrying broom, with carrying broom."

"How did you get such small small arms?"
(*whiningly*) "Aih-h-h!—late—and *wee-e-e*—moul."

"How did you get such huge huge hands?"
(*gruffly*) "Threshing with an iron flail, threshing with an iron flail."

"How did you get such a small small neck?"
(*pitifully*) "Aih-h-h!—late—and *wee-e-e*—moul."

"How did you get such a huge huge head?"
(*keenly*) "Much knowledge, much knowledge."

"What did you come for?"
(*at the top of the voice, with a wave of the arm and a stamp of the feet*) "FOR YOU!"

DIRECTIONS

This is a mysterious and powerful story. I have given it exactly as it is printed in Joseph Jacobs' *English Folk and Fairy Tales*. Of the meaning of "Aih-h-h—late—and wee-e-e—moul," Jacobs states, "I candidly confess I have not the slightest idea what it means; judging other children by myself, I do not think that makes the response less effective."[†]

This story is certainly worth the trouble of memorizing the words, cutting out all the separate pieces of the "strange visitor," and practicing using different voices for the characters. Place the pieces in order very carefully before beginning the story.

Participation

Pass out the pieces of the "strange visitor" to the children: one child will have a piece or pair of pieces that go with one stanza. That child will be responsible for adding her piece(s) to the "strange visitor" on the flannel board at the correct time, and also for giving the visitor's answer to the woman's question about that part of his body later in the poem.

[†] Joseph Jacobs, *English Folk and Fairy Tales* (G.P. Putnam's, 1907), p. 271.

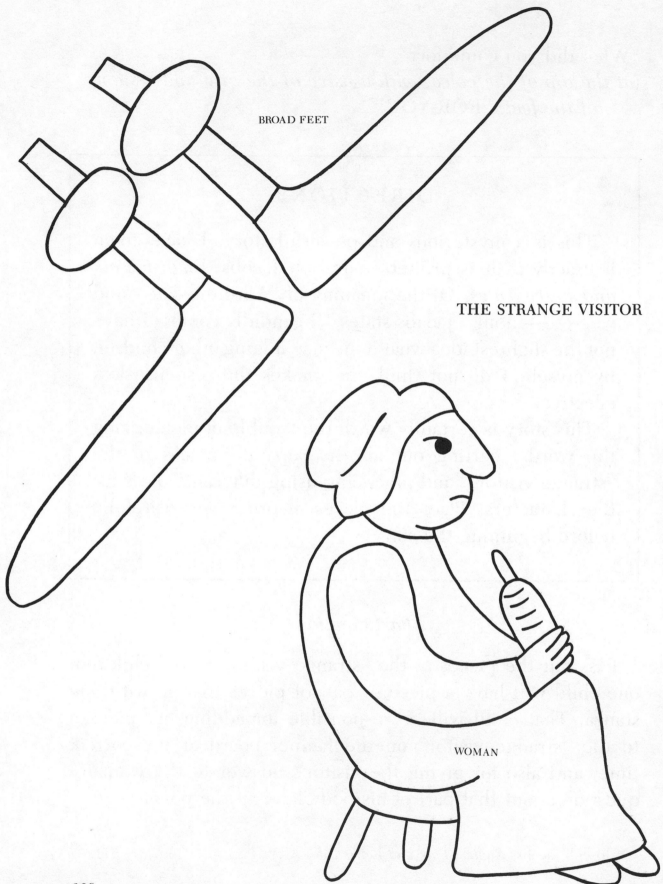

BROAD FEET

THE STRANGE VISITOR

WOMAN

138

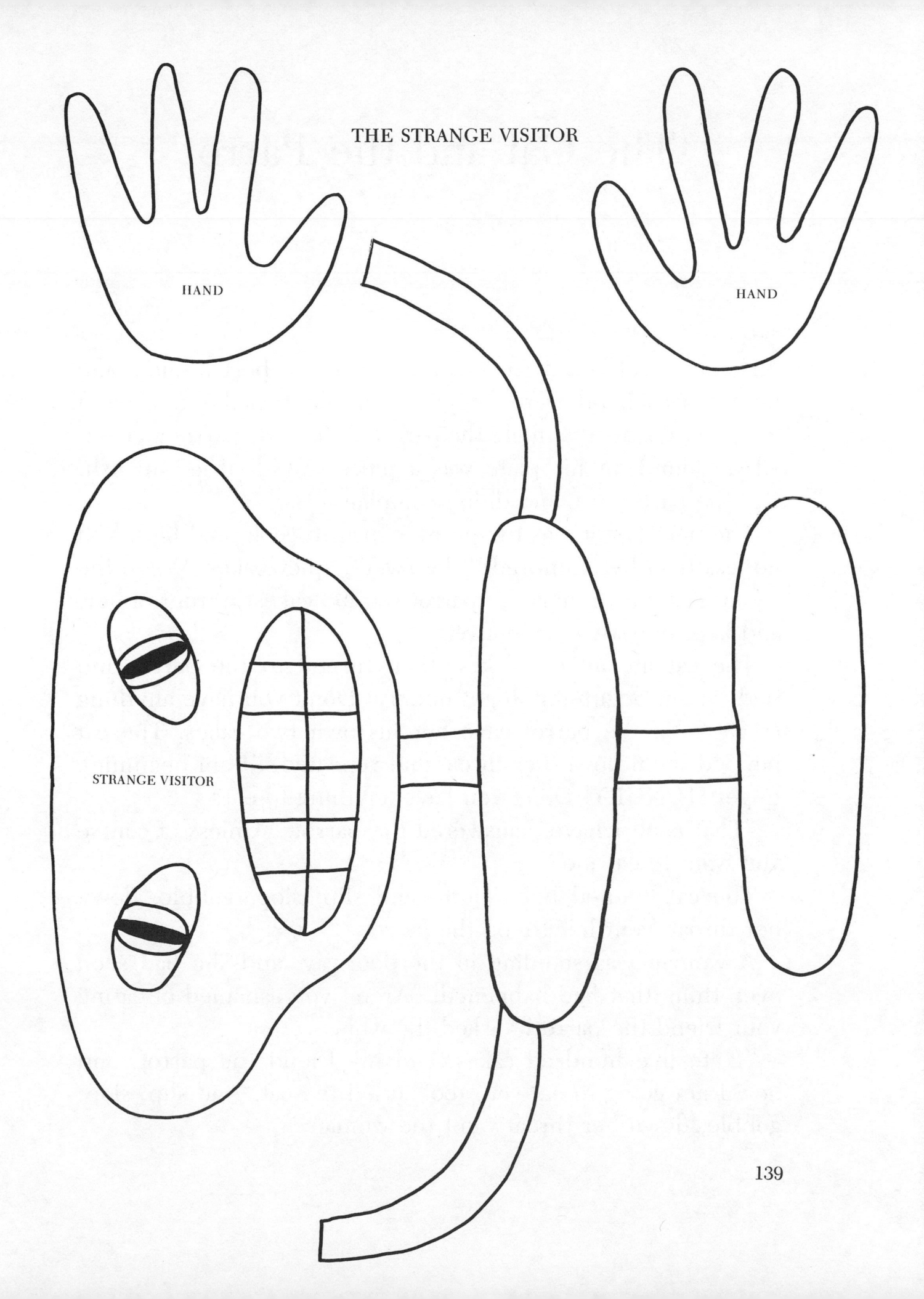

THE STRANGE VISITOR

HAND

HAND

STRANGE VISITOR

139

The Cat and the Parrot

AN INDIAN TALE

Once, a cat and a parrot promised to be best friends, and to invite each other to dinner, turn and turnabout. First it was the cat's turn to invite the parrot. When the parrot arrived, all he found on his plate was a piece of old, dried-up fish. But the parrot ate, and didn't complain.

The next day it was the parrot's turn to cook, and he baked no less than five hundred little, sweet, spicy cakes. When the cat arrived for dinner, the parrot set 498 cakes in front of her, and kept only two for himself.

The cat ate all the cakes, then turned to the parrot and said, "I am beginning to get hungry! Don't you have anything to eat?" So the parrot gave her his own two cakes. The cat popped them down her throat and repeated, "I am beginning to get HUNGRY! Don't you have anything to eat?"

"That is all I have," answered the parrot. "Unless of course you want to eat me."

The cat opened her mouth, and slip, slop, gobble, down her throat went her friend the parrot.

A woman was standing in the doorway, and she had seen everything that had happened. "Aren't you ashamed of eating your friend the parrot?" asked the woman.

"I ate five hundred cakes, and my friend the parrot, and now I am going to eat you, too!" cried the cat. And slip, slop, gobble, down her throat went the woman.*

The cat, who was now quite fat, began to walk down the street. She met a man who was beating his donkey, trying to make the poor beast trot faster.

"Watch out, kitty cat," cried the man, "or my donkey will step on you."

"Step on me?" cried the cat. "I ate five hundred cakes, and my friend the parrot, and a meddlesome woman, and now I am going to eat you, too!" And down the cat's throat went the man and the donkey, slip, slop, gobble!

The cat turned onto the main street, and coming toward her she saw the king, riding on his favorite elephant.

"Look out, kitty cat!" called the king. "My elephant might trample you."

"Trample me, indeed!" cried the cat. "I ate five hundred cakes, and my friend the parrot, and a meddlesome woman, and a man and his donkey, and now I am going to eat you, too!" And slip, slop, gobble, down the cat's throat went the king and the elephant.

The cat turned to walk toward the beach, and she met two land crabs, scuttling along with their claws waving in the air.

"Move aside! Move aside! Coming through!" shouted the land crabs.

"Move aside, indeed!" cried the cat. "I ate five hundred cakes, and my friend the parrot, and a meddlesome woman, and a man and his donkey, and the king and his elephant, and now I am going to eat you for dessert." And slip, slop, gobble, down the cat's throat went the two land crabs.**

Now this is what the land crabs saw when they reached the cat's stomach: In one corner, the sad, bedraggled parrot sat on a pile of five hundred cakes. Next to the parrot sat the woman, still scolding, "Aren't you ashamed of yourself?" In another corner, the man was still beating his donkey, and on the other side of the cat's stomach, the king had fainted and the elephant was fanning him with its trunk, trying to revive him.

The two land crabs looked at each other and said, "Let's get to work!" And snip! snip! snip! snip! they cut a hole in the cat's stomach, and out came the two land crabs, the old woman (still scolding the cat), the man (still beating his donkey), the king (his elephant carried him on its trunk), and, last of all, the parrot, holding a little sweet spicy cake in each claw (that was all he wanted in the first place, remember?).

And as for the cat, she borrowed a needle and thread, and spent the rest of the day sewing up that hole in her stomach.

Follow-up

Act the story out in creative dramatics. One child is the cat (you can paint whiskers on her). Tie a large bedsheet or a thin bedspread around that child's neck, like a giant bib. As the cat eats each story character, the child playing that character gets under the sheet. At **, instead of *seeing* inside the cat's stomach, we *hear* each of them complaining inside the stomach. Each actor can make up her own lines at this point. At the end, everyone emerges and the cat mimes sewing up the hole in her stomach.

DIRECTIONS

This story is a bit complicated to present on the flannel board, but it is great fun and well worth the effort. Most characters go on and off the flannel board twice during the story, so you will have to practice keeping them in the right order. As you remove characters that have been eaten, do it roughly, by grabbing them.

At *, substitute the fatter cat for the original. At **, the scene shifts to a view inside the cat's stomach (a sort of x-ray view). Remove the cat from the board and place each other character back on the board as you tell about it. To show the characters coming out of the cat's stomach, lift each carefully off the flannel board and show it to the children before placing it in your lap. When the board is empty again, place the original cat figure there as you tell about her sewing up the hole in her stomach.

CAT

CAKES

WOMAN

FAT CAT

THE CAT AND THE PARROT

KING

PARROT

FISH PLATTER

CAKES

144

ELEPHANT

THE CAT AND THE PARROT

DONKEY

MAN

CRABS

145

The Fish with the Deep Sea Smile

A POEM BY MARGARET WISE BROWN

They fished and they fished
Way down in the sea,
Down in the sea a mile.
They fished among all the fish in the sea,
For the fish with the deep sea smile.

One fish came up from the deep of the sea,
From down in the sea a mile,
It had blue-green eyes
And whiskers three
But never a deep sea smile.

One fish came from the deep of the sea,
From down in the sea a mile,
With electric lights up and down his tail
But never a deep sea smile.

They fished and they fished
Way down in the sea,
Down in the sea a mile.
They fished among all the fish in the sea,
For the fish with a deep sea smile.

One fish came up with terrible teeth,
One fish with long strong jaws,
One fish came up with long stalked eyes,
One fish with terrible claws.*

They fished all through the ocean deep,
For many and many a mile.
And they caught a fish with a laughing eye,
But none with a deep sea smile.

And then one day they got a pull,
From down in the sea a mile.
And when they pulled the fish into the boat,
He smiled a deep sea smile.

And as he smiled the hook got free,
And then, what a deep sea smile!
He flipped his tail and swam away,
Down in the sea a mile.

Follow-up

Act the poem out in creative dramatics: fishermen will sit together while fish swim around the room. Decide together how the children will use their hands, bodies, and facial expressions to act out each of the fish characters. Practice the mime of each fish taking the bait and being reeled in by one of the fishermen. Then read the poem, pausing for action by the children.

DIRECTIONS

Patterns are given for the fishermen in their boat and for the eight fish mentioned in the poem. However, the children can make their own fish for the story, and even add others, complete with descriptive names, added at the *.

FISHERMEN AND BOAT

WHISKERED FISH

TERRIBLE TEETH FISH

FISH WITH THE DEEP SEA SMILE

ELECTRIC FISH

149

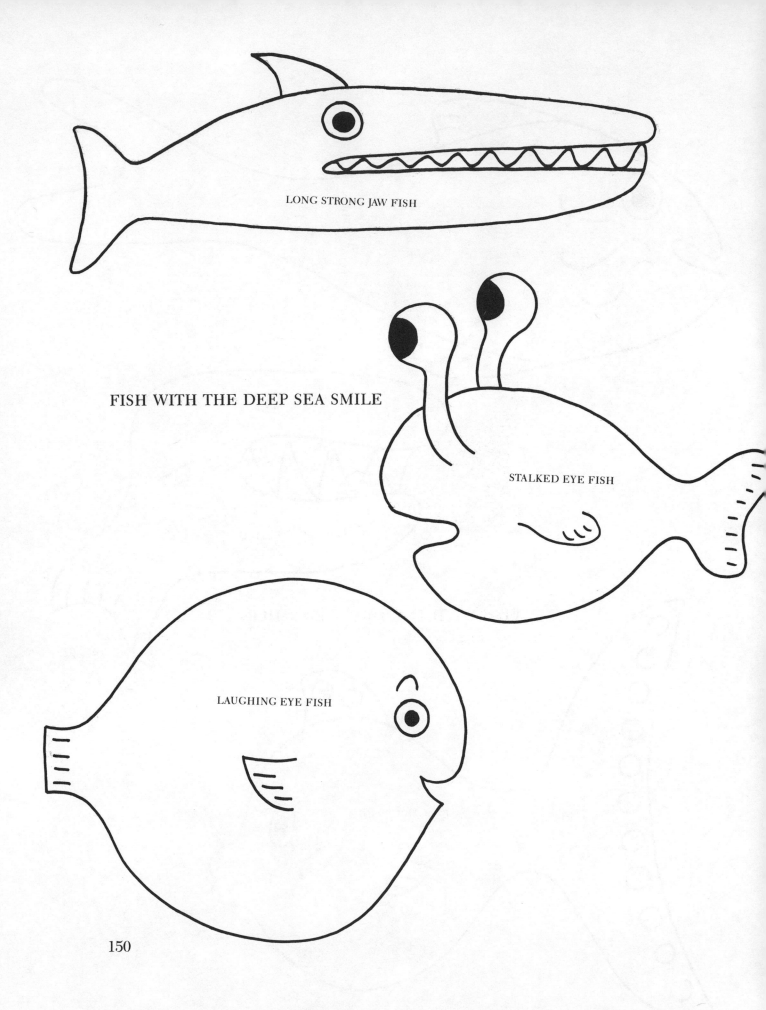

LONG STRONG JAW FISH

FISH WITH THE DEEP SEA SMILE

STALKED EYE FISH

LAUGHING EYE FISH

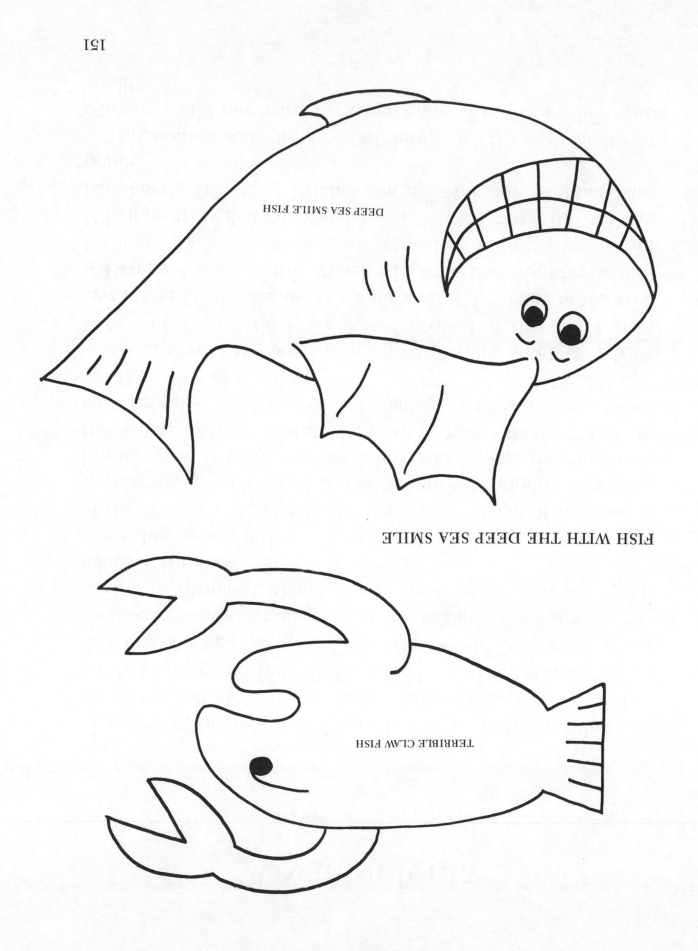

151

DEEP SEA SMILE FISH

FISH WITH THE DEEP SEA SMILE

TERRIBLE CLAW FISH

Uwungelema

AN AFRICAN (BANTU) TALE

THERE WAS a famine in the land, and the only crop that was not destroyed by drought was the fruit of a certain large tree. As that fruit grew ripe, all the animals gathered around. Now, this was a magic tree, and the fruit would only drop when someone said the name of the tree out loud. The animals realized with dismay that not one of them could remember the name of the tree!

So they sent the hare off to see the king, to get the name of the tree. The king told the hare, "The name of the tree is Uwungelema!" The hare ran back quickly, hoppity skippety, but when he arrived at the tree, he could not exactly remember the name. "Olonganewa," he said. "Malongabema." But no fruit dropped, and the animals had to send someone else to get the name of the tree.

Eland went. He was swift, and he could surely get back before he forgot the word. Eland arrived at the king's kraal and asked for the name. The king said, "The name of the tree is Uwungelema!" Swiftly the eland darted back, but he twisted his foot—ouch!—and the surprise made him forget the name. When he arrived at the tree, he said, "Uwelawela." But nothing happened. He said, "Ulongawonga." But still nothing happened.

The animals were hungry and desperate. If their two fastest runners could not bring back the name of the tree, then who could?

152

"I would like to try," said Tortoise.

"I don't think we can wait that long," said Hare.

"You will have to," said Tortoise, and he set off on his journey, which lasted two days and two nights, and Tortoise never slept.

When Tortoise arrived at the kraal of the king, he asked, "What is the name of the tree?"

"The name of the tree is Uwungelema," replied the king.

Tortoise asked again, and a third time, and each time the king repeated the name: Uwungelema.

All the way back, the tortoise repeated the name of the tree: Uwungelema, Uwungelema, Uwungelema.

When he stepped on a thorn, he did not stop saying Uwungelema. When a horsefly bit him, he did not stop saying Uwungelema. When a branch fell on him, he did not stop saying Uwungelema.

When he reached the tree, he said the name Uwungelema loud and clear, and the fruits dropped down one by one to the hungry animals, and there was enough fruit to keep them through the time of famine, thanks to the tortoise.

Follow-up

This is one of many stories of "slow and steady wins the race"—and one of the most satisfying. It can lead to a discussion of how to remember difficult words and numbers, always an important matter for young children.

DIRECTIONS

Make the hare, eland, and tortoise of interfacing, and color them on both sides. Cut the tree from felt, and cut separate fruits to place on it. The tree goes in the lower left of the flannel board. Hare, Eland, and Tortoise cluster about the base of the tree. Place King Lion in the upper right of the board. Hare and Eland travel to see the king in several leaps. Tortoise travels slowly—you may even drag him along as you narrate his journey.

The magic word is pronounced "Oo-won-guh-LAY-muh."

When the tortoise says the name of the tree, lift the fruits off the tree and place them next to the animals.

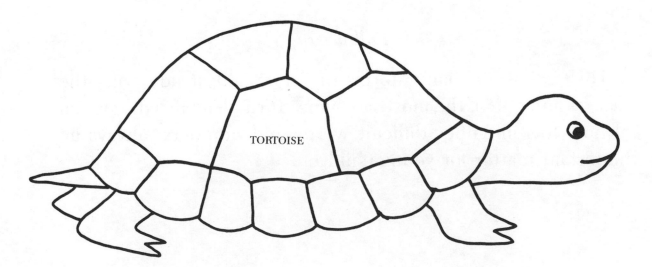

TORTOISE

UWUNGELEMA

KING LION

HARE

UWUNGELEMA

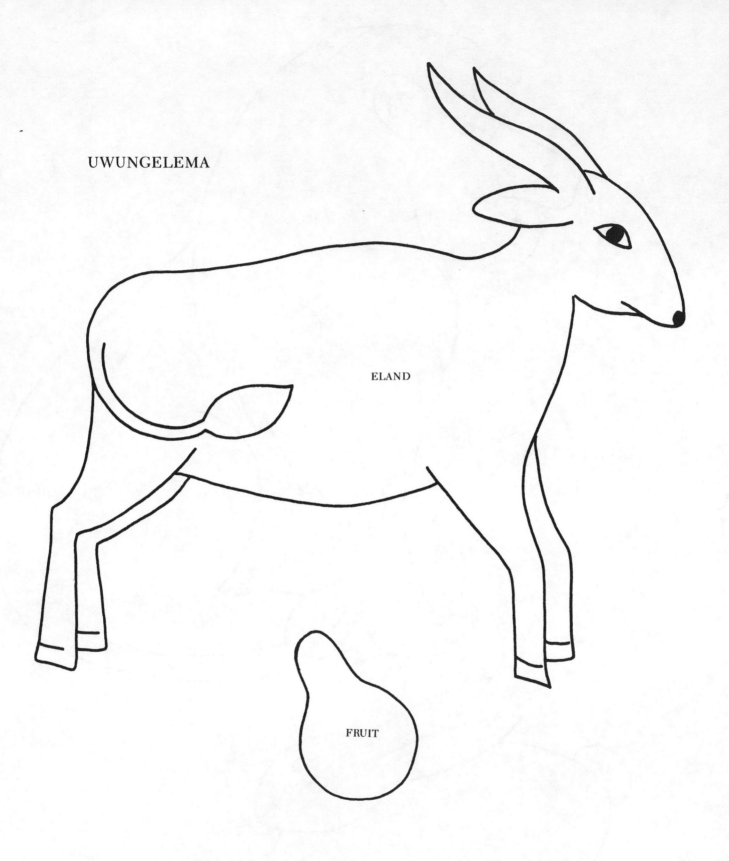

ELAND

FRUIT

156

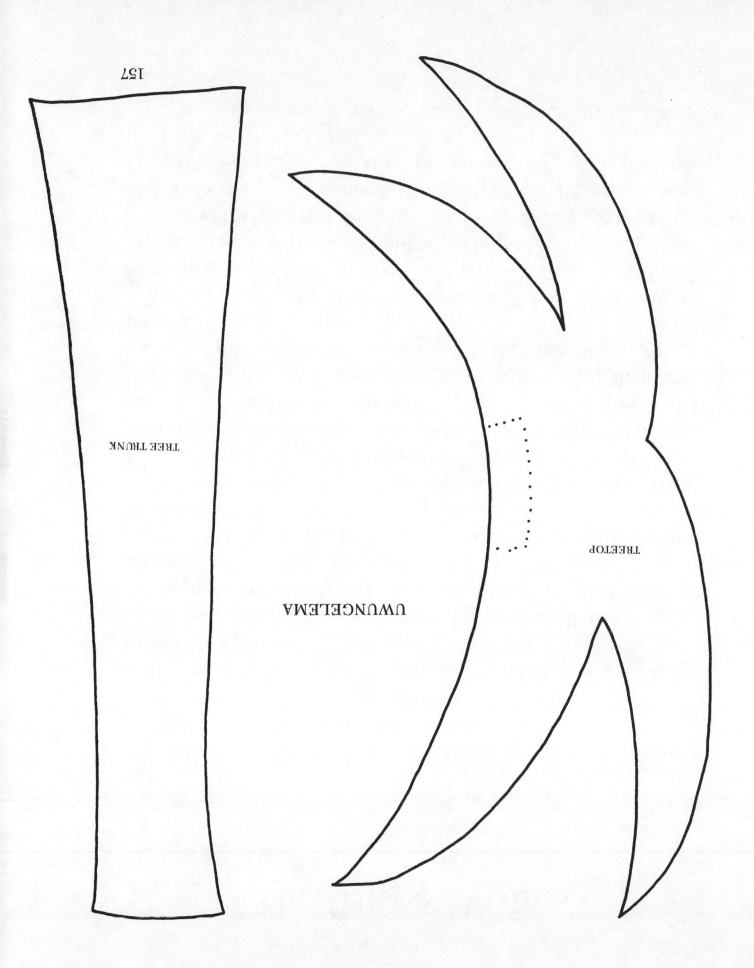

157

TREE TRUNK

UWUNGELMA

TREETOP

The Three Wishes

A GERMAN TALE

A MAN went to cut wood in the forest one day. He chose a gnarled old oak tree, and raised his axe.

"No! No!" came a wee small voice.

The man looked around, and as he didn't see a soul, he raised his axe again.*

"Please, spare this tree!" came the wee small voice again.

The man looked up and saw a tiny little elf, all dressed in green, almost hidden amongst the leaves of the tree.

"This tree is my home. Please don't be chopping it down," begged the elf.

The man laughed at the sight of such a tiny creature. "Well, I would never chop down a person's home," said he.

"Indeed, and you have done better for yourself today than you think," said the wee small elf. "For I know magic, and I shall grant your next three wishes, no matter what they be."

As the man started to thank the elf, the little fellow disappeared.**

The man hurried home to tell his wife of their good fortune, but when he arrived, she was not in the house. "Oh dear," said the man in a low voice, talking to himself, "I am so hungry . . . how I wish I had a great, fat sausage here right now!"

And to the man's astonishment—ZIP!—the biggest sausage he had ever seen appeared on the table. And just at that moment, in walked his wife.

"What's this? You home so early, and such an enormous

158

sausage on the table! Where ever did it come from?" she asked.

The man had to tell her all about the old oak tree and the wee small elf and the three wishes.

"And so!" cried the wife. "You have wasted one of our three precious wishes on a sausage? I wish that sausage were stuck on the end of your nose, for all the world to see what a simpleton you are!"

And—ZIP!—the sausage rose up off the table and—ZAP!—it stuck fast to the top of the poor man's nose.

"Now look! You've gone and wasted our second wish!" cried the man. "Get this sausage OFF MY NOSE!"

The woman grabbed hold of the sausage and pulled, and pulled, but pull as she might, the sausage was stuck tight on the end of her husband's nose.

"Give me your axe, then, and I'll chop it off," said the woman.

"No!" shouted the man.

"Well, then, you shall just have to learn to live with it," said the wife. "And it doesn't look so bad, either. When we use our third wish to get heaps of money, we can tie it all up in silk ribbons."

"No," said the man. "I want it off my nose, and I want it off now!"

The woman tried long and hard to persuade the husband that sacks full of gold were well worth a sausage on the nose. Finally, she exclaimed angrily, "Oh, I wish that sausage were off your nose and this whole trouble finished!"

And—PLOP!—the sausage dropped off the man's nose onto the table. That was the end of their three wishes, and all they got for it was a sausage and an argument.

DIRECTIONS

Cut the tree from colored felt: brown for the trunk and green for the leaves. Glue each green piece to the proper side of the tree trunk, following the letters on the pattern, but do not glue the green pieces together. Before the children see the flannel board, set up the tree in the center of the board, lapping the left green piece over the right one. Hide the elf under the left green piece so that just the tip of his hat, his nose, and his toes show. At *, pull the elf out so that his whole elf self can be seen.

At **, remove the elf and the tree. Leave the man where he is, and place the table just to his left. The wife will stand to the left of the table and when she pulls on the sausage, move her so that her hand is on top of it.

Follow-up

This story is a great discussion starter: What would you wish for? Could you live with a sausage on your nose? Do wishes ever come true?

SAUSAGE

THE THREE WISHES

TREE TRUNK

MAN

161

ARCADIA PUBLIC LIBRARY
ARCADIA, WISCONSIN 54612

TABLE

THE THREE WISHES

WIFE

TREETOP

B   C

THE THREE WISHES

TREETOP

A

ELF

The Elf and the Dormouse

A POEM BY OLIVER HEREFORD

Under a toadstool
   Crept a wee Elf.
Out of the rain
   To shelter himself.

Under the toadstool,
   Sound asleep,
Sat a big Dormouse
   All in a heap.

Trembled the wee Elf,
   Frightened, and yet
Fearing to fly away
   Lest he got wet.

To the next shelter—
   Maybe a mile!
Sudden the wee Elf
   Smiled a wee smile.

Tugged till the toadstool
   Toppled in two.
Holding it over him,
   Gaily he flew.

Soon he was safe home,
   Dry as could be.

Soon woke the Dormouse—
"Good gracious me!"

"Where is my toadstool?"
Loud he lamented.
And that's how umbrellas
First were invented.

DIRECTIONS

Cut the toadstool of felt or interfacing, and cut the stem along the line shown on the pattern. Place it to the left of center of the flannel board. Overlap the two pieces slightly so that the cut is not obvious. Cut the dormouse's tail along the dotted line and place him to the right of the toadstool. Cover his eye with the furry end of his tail to make him look as if he is asleep (you will take the tail off the eye later, when he wakes up).

The elf is placed to the left of the toadstool, just as you begin the poem. When he tugs "till the toadstool/ Toppled in two. . . ," you pick up the elf and "umbrella" and place them in the upper right for the rest of the poem.

Follow-up

Ask the children if they can think of some other ingenious "inventions from nature" along the same line as the elf's use of the toadstool as an umbrella.

TOADSTOOL

THE ELF
AND THE DORMOUSE

DORMOUSE

ELF

166

Rattlesnake, Mouse, and Coyote

A MEXICAN TALE

Mouse was running across the mesa, scurrying between the stones, looking for seeds to eat.

"Help! Help!" A tiny voice, faraway and muffled, called from under a nearby rock. Mouse stopped running and listened. "Please let me out!" the voice cried. "Roll this stone over and let me out!"

Mouse pushed the rock with his paws and nudged it with his nose. At last, the rock rolled aside. Out came Rattlesnake, hissing and shaking his tail rattles. As soon as he saw Mouse, he grabbed Mouse tightly in his coils.

"Let me go!" cried Mouse. "It was I who moved the rock aside to let you out. I saved your life."

"You saved my life because you are a kindhearted mouse. I am going to eat you because I am a hungry rattlesnake," Rattlesnake replied.

"But you should be grateful and spare my life. If it weren't for me, you would still be trapped under that rock."

"Rattlesnakes are not grateful," said the rattlesnake.

Just then, Señor Coyote came trotting along. "Hey! Cousin!" cried Mouse. "Is this fair? I saved Rattlesnake's life, and now he is going to eat me."

"What?" asked Coyote. "How did this happen?"

"Rattlesnake was trapped in a hole under that rock," said Mouse. "I rolled the rock aside and let him out. I saved his life, and now he wants to eat me."

"No one says rattlesnakes have to be grateful," said Rattlesnake. "I'm hungry, because I was under that rock for so long."

"I don't understand. This doesn't make sense," said Coyote. "You say Mouse was under the rock?"

"No, I was under the rock!" hissed Rattlesnake.

"Oh, my poor brains," said Coyote. "I can't understand at all. . . . Rattlesnake rolled the rock off Mouse. . . ."

"NO! Mouse rolled the rock off me!"

"I just can't understand at all. Please be so kind as to show me exactly what happened."

"I was in here," said Rattlesnake, letting go of Mouse and crawling back into the hole.

"And this rock was on top of you?" asked Coyote, pushing the rock back on top of Rattlesnake.

"Yes! Yes! Now let me out!" came Rattlesnake's small voice from under the rock.

"I will leave that up to Mouse," answered Coyote as he trotted away.

DIRECTIONS

Cut the rock from felt and place it so it completely covers Rattlesnake before the children see the flannel board. When Mouse pushes the rock aside, pull the felt rock off Rattlesnake and place it to one side, still on the flannel board. Put Rattlesnake on top of Mouse so that it looks as if Mouse is caught in Rattlesnake's coils. When Rattlesnake gets back into the "hole," simply put him in the place he was originally, then cover him with the felt rock.

Follow-up

This is a classic trickster tale, with variants found around the world. It can be used to start a lively discussion of what Mouse should have done to avoid being captured, and whether or not Rattlesnake should have been grateful.

RATTLESNAKE, MOUSE, AND COYOTE

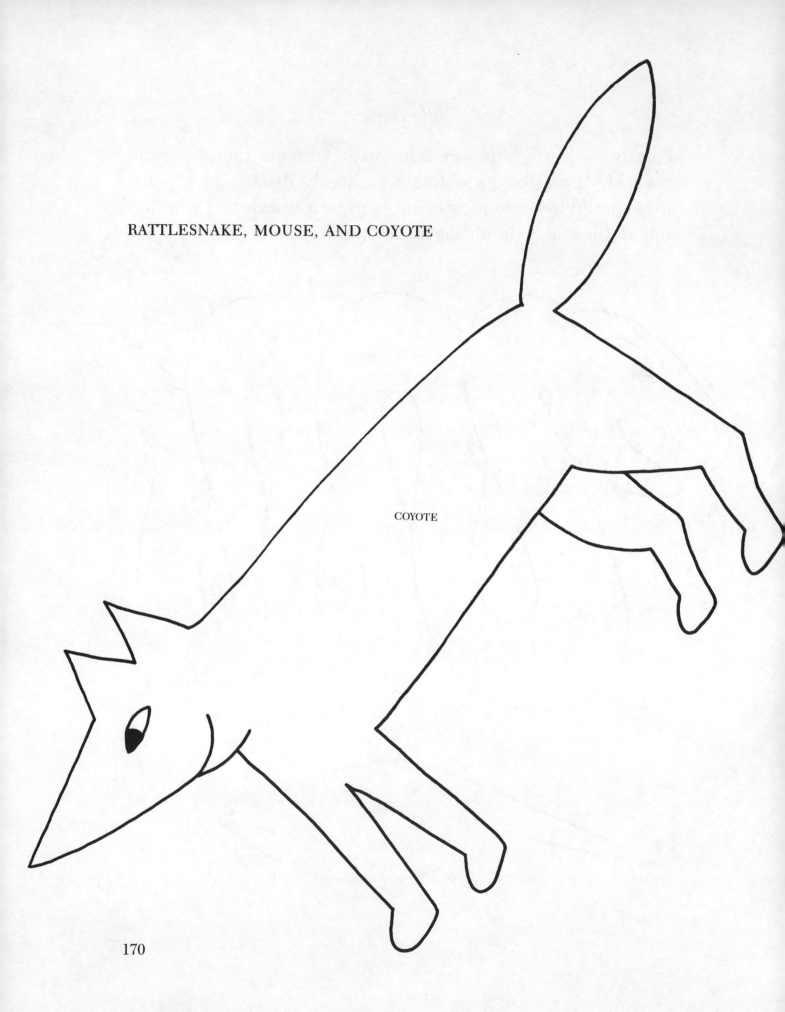

COYOTE

170

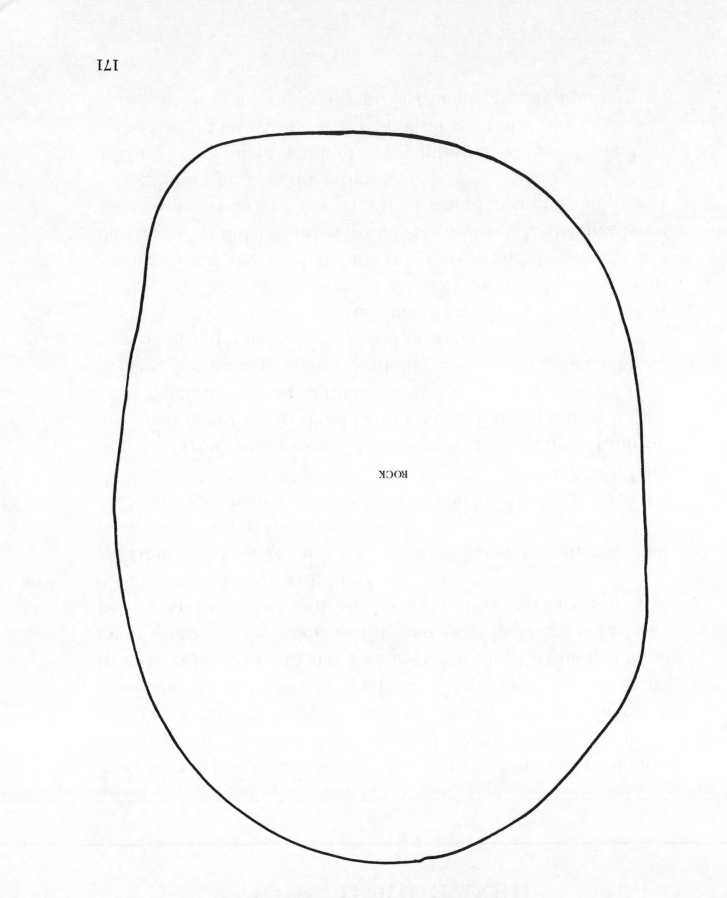

ROCK

RATTLESNAKE, MOUSE, AND COYOTE

Soup from a Nail

A SWEDISH TALE

ONE EVENING an old woman was sitting alone in her house. She heard a knock at the door, and when she opened it, in came a ragged old beggar man. She asked him where he came from and what it was he wanted. He replied that he came from South-of-the-Sun and East-of-the-Moon, that he had been everywhere in the wide world, and now he was on his way home. And could she please be so kind as to share a morsel of something to eat with him?

"How can I share with you, when I haven't even any food for myself!" cried the woman.

"Why, you poor creature!" exclaimed the beggar. "Then I shall have to ask you to share my supper." He pulled a long iron nail from his pocket. "I have used this many a time on my travels, but there should still be some magic left in it."

"A magic nail?" asked the woman.

"Yes, for making soup," said the man. "Would you be so kind as to fetch me a large kettle of water?"

The woman fetched a kettle, filled it with water, and put it on the fire. The beggar turned the nail around three times in his hand and dropped it into the water, and began stirring slowly. "It could be quite weak," he muttered, "having been used so much lately. Yes, an onion would certainly help. But we shall just have to do without."

Then the woman suddenly remembered where she had an onion tucked away, and it was soon in the pot.

"A wealthy man I stayed with last month insisted on putting

172

some carrots and beets into the soup, but of course, that is not necessary for simple folk like us," said the beggar.

The woman searched and managed to find some carrots and beets, which soon joined the onion rolling in the kettle.

"And of course, when I made this magic soup for the king, he insisted on some oatmeal for thickening, and some salt and spices for taste, though these things won't be necessary for simple folk like us." The beggar smiled at the woman and winked.

"No, no," she insisted, "I should like to taste it exactly as the king tasted it." And she brought out oatmeal, salt, and herbs, letting them fall into the pot as the man stirred.

When at last the soup was ready,* the woman spread her best cloth on the table and brought out a bottle of wine. When she tasted the soup, she declared that she could scarcely believe that it had been made from just one ordinary-looking nail!

DIRECTIONS

This is a simple story to tell with the flannel board. Cut the pot from felt. As the nail and other ingredients are added to the pot, simply place them on top of it, as if we could see through it. At *, remove the pot and replace it with the table.

Follow-up

This story gives you and the children a perfect excuse to make nail soup together. Don't forget to remove the nail before serving! Pretend as you eat the soup that it is, truly, magic. . . then discuss what kinds of real and ordinary events can seem magical.

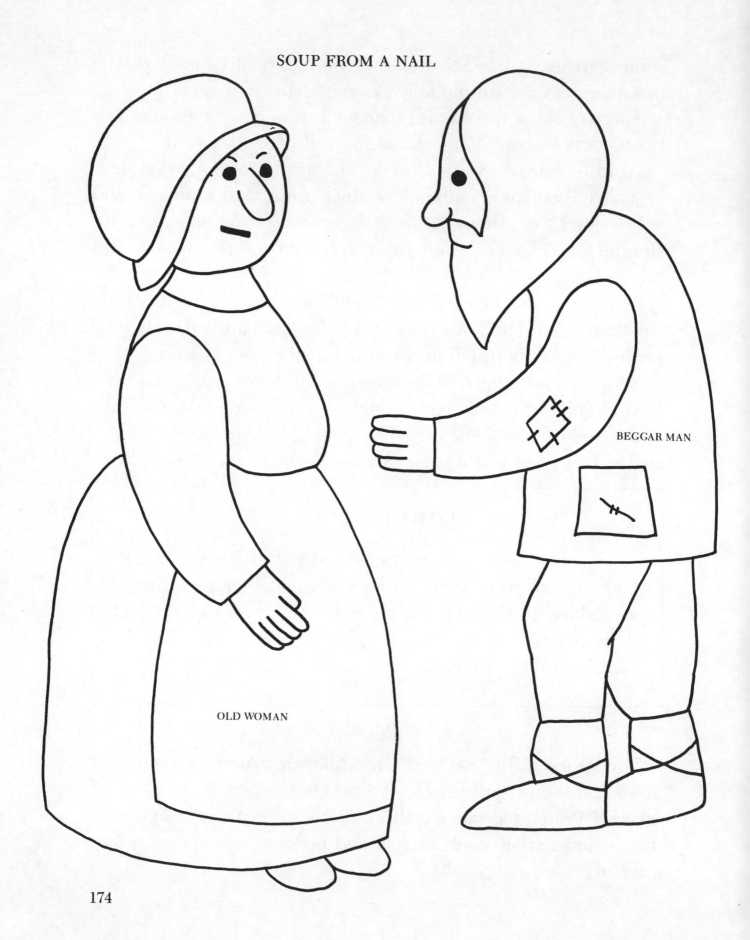

OLD WOMAN

BEGGAR MAN

174

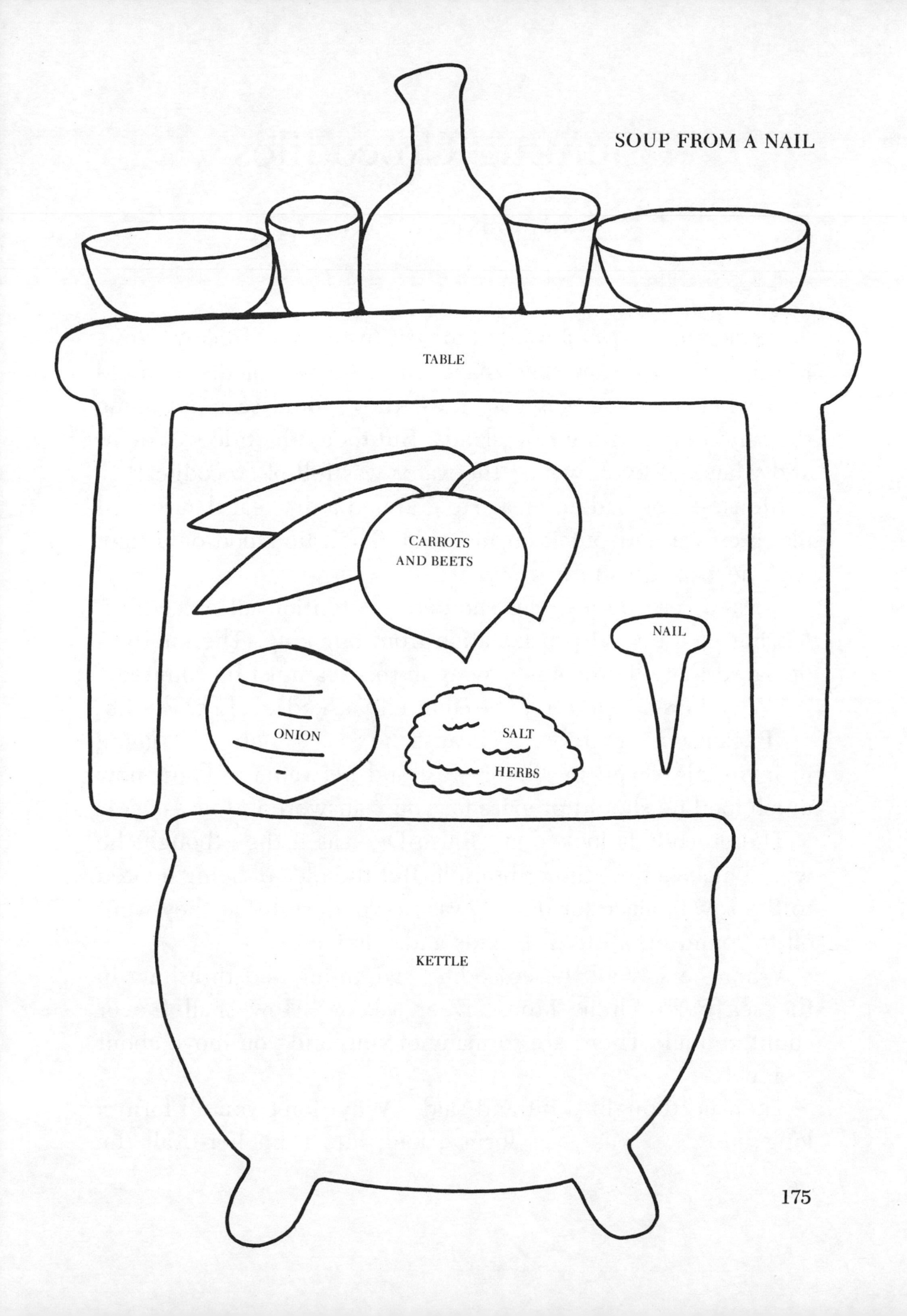

TABLE

CARROTS
AND BEETS

NAIL

ONION

SALT

HERBS

KETTLE

Counting Crocodiles

AN INDONESIAN TALE

ONCE, MOUSE-DEER wanted to visit his friend Monkey. Now, Monkey lived on another island, and the two of them would visit when the tide was very low—they would scamper along the sand between the two islands. But today the tide was high, and what was even worse, the water was full of crocodiles!*

Mouse-Deer had an idea. He grabbed a dry leaf that looked like a crown and put it on his head. Then he stood on a high rock next to the shore.

"Listen, crocodiles!" he shouted. "Attention all crocodiles. I bring you a royal proclamation from our king. The king has declared that all crocodiles living in this sea must be counted!"

"Why does he want us to be counted?" asked an old crocodile.

"Because . . . oh . . . because he is . . . uh . . . going to invite all of you to dinner, yes, and he wants to know how much food he should prepare for you," answered Mouse-Deer.

The crocodiles looked at Mouse-Deer as if they thought he would make a fine dinner himself. But the idea of being invited to the royal palace for dinner was so wonderful that they went off to round up all their friends and relatives.**

When he saw all the crocodiles swimming and thrashing in the sea before him, Mouse-Deer asked, "How shall I ever count you all? There are so many of you, and you move about so much."

Then he thought a bit and said, "Why don't you all form a long line . . . yes . . . form a long line from here, all the

176

way to that island over there. Then I will be able to count you."

The crocodiles formed a long line, head to tail, stretching from the place where Mouse-Deer stood all the way to the island. Mouse-Deer then jumped from crocodile to crocodile, counting as he went, "One, two, three, four, five, six, seven. . . ." Then he hopped off the last crocodile and onto the island.

"You will all be receiving your dinner invitations soon!" he called out to the crocodiles. "Good bye!"

Then Mouse-Deer trotted into the jungle to find his friend Monkey.

DIRECTIONS

Cut seven crocodiles, or as many as will make an overlapping diagonal line across your flannel board. Make the old crocodile slightly different from the rest—a lighter color or draw in some wrinkles. To mark off the shores of the sea, cut two triangles of tan felt, about 4″ wide and 2″ high, and place one at the lower right and one in the upper left of the flannel board. Mouse-Deer is in the lower right corner as the story begins.

At *, place three crocodiles on the flannel board, and at **, place the rest on. When they form a line, place them in a row from shore to shore, overlapping them if necessary. Pick up Mouse-Deer and hop him from crocodile to crocodile as you count.

Follow-up

Act out the story as a group. Use a hand puppet for Mouse-Deer (any furry animal can be renamed for the occasion) and have all the children be crocodiles. The width of the room can be the water, or you can use chairs or tables to mark the two shores.

Tell the story, you or a child playing the part of Mouse-Deer with the puppet. At the end, have a crocodile bridge across the room. Touch the puppet to each child's head, then the next, counting as you go.

Be sure you coach the children in feeling and acting like crocodiles. How do the crocodiles feel when they realize that they have been tricked? How do they show their feelings?

LEAF

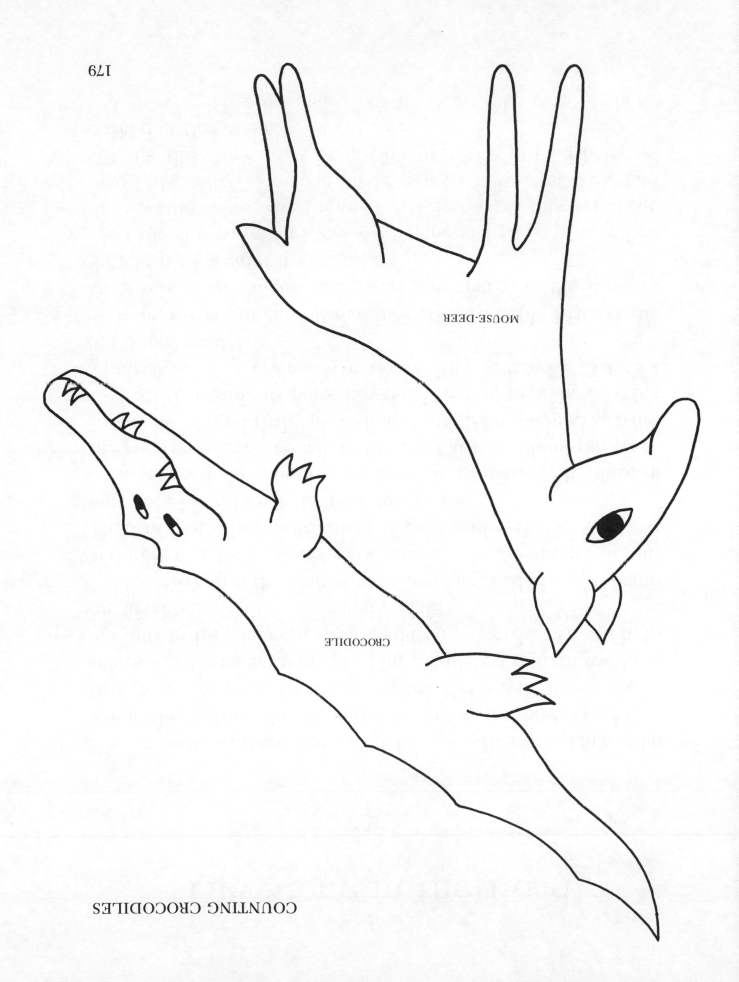

MOUSE-DEER

CROCODILE

COUNTING CROCODILES

The Stone in the Road

ORIGIN UNKNOWN

A CERTAIN country was ruled by a kindhearted king, who would do anything for his subjects. But at last he noticed that they were growing lazy, and seldom did anything for themselves—or for each other! The king wondered if there was anyone left in his kingdom who would go out of his way to help his neighbors. So he concocted a plan.

Late one night, the king went to the main road of the kingdom and rolled a huge stone right smack into the middle of it. Then he secretly placed a bag of gold under the stone. Next morning, he hid near the road to watch.

First, a woman came by on her way to market. Because of the stone, she had to walk in the mud at the side of the road. "Someone should really move that stone," she snapped angrily.

Next, two students passed by on their way to school. "What a nuisance!" they cried. "Why doesn't the king move that rock out of our road?"

And so it continued all day long: some people blamed the king, some blamed the stone, and some even hit the stone as they walked around it.

As the sun was about to set, a young girl passed by. When she saw the stone, she stopped. "I'd better get this out of the road," she said. "Someone might pass by here after dark, and not see the stone, and bump into it." The girl pushed and pushed at the stone.

A man walking by said, "Let the king take care of that."

But the girl kept pushing until at last the stone began to roll, and rolled over the edge of the road and down a hill.

It was then that she saw the bag of gold the king had left there.

Everyone agreed that the girl deserved the gold. And, everyone was more than a little bit ashamed that they had not thought of moving the stone. After that, they began helping each other instead of waiting for the king to do things for them.

DIRECTIONS

Place a length of yarn or a ½" strip of felt across the middle of the flannel board to represent the road. When the king "hides," place him in the lower left corner of the board.

Follow-up

This makes for good creative drama, with an imaginary rock, taller than the children. After choosing the king and the little girl (or boy), either let the other children make up their own characters of people in the kingdom, or give each of them a slip of paper with a character's name on it. Let each decide how she or he will react to the stone.

Practice running into the stone, feeling it, and walking around it, to give reality to the drama.

GOLD

STUDENTS

THE STONE IN THE ROAD

GIRL

KING

182

STONE

WOMAN

MAN

THE STONE IN THE ROAD

183

Peace and Quiet

A YIDDISH TALE

ONCE, A man lived all alone in a little house. He had a good farm with cows and horses, pigs and chickens. But he was very unhappy because he could never, ever get any peace and quiet. The door in his little house creaked. The floorboards next to his little bed squeaked, and the windows rattled all night long.

With all that creaking and squeaking and rattling, the man could never even get a good night's sleep. So he went to see the wise woman. The wise woman listened to his story and thought for a while, and then asked, "Do you have a chicken?"

"Yes, I have many chickens," the man answered.

"Tonight, bring a chicken into the house," advised the wise woman.

The man went home and took a chicken into his little house. That night, the door creaked, the floorboards squeaked, the windows rattled, and the chicken cackled. The man got even less sleep than before!

So the next day, he went once again to see the wise woman. "Oh, Wise Woman," he moaned, "I did what you told me. I took a chicken into my house, and now the noise is worse than before."

The wise woman listened and nodded, and thought for a while, and then she asked, "Do you have a pig?"

"Yes," answered the man, "I have many pigs."

"Tonight, bring a pig into the house," said the wise woman.

The man went home and took a pig into his little house.

That night, the door creaked, the floorboards squeaked, the windows rattled, the chicken cackled, and the pig grunted. The man lay awake the whole night with his eyes open.

The next day, he went once again to see the wise woman. "Wise Woman!" he cried. "I did what you told me. I took a pig into my house. The noise is now unbearable!"

The wise woman listened, and thought for a while, and then she asked, "Do you have a cow?"

"Yes," the man answered, "I have several cows."

"Tonight," advised the wise woman, "bring a cow into the house."

The man went home and took a cow into his little house. That night, the door creaked, the floorboards squeaked, the windows rattled, the chicken cackled, the pig grunted, and the cow mooed. The man spent the whole night sitting on the edge of his bed, holding his ears and moaning.

The next day, he went once again to see the wise woman. "Wise Woman," he whimpered, "I did what you told me. I took a cow into my house. Now I can no longer sleep. How can a man live if he does not sleep?"

The wise woman listened, and thought for a while, and looked at the man, and asked, "Do you have a horse?"

"I know, I know," said the man, and he returned home.

That night, the man took a horse into his little house. He lay down on the bed and listened. The door creaked, the floorboards squeaked, the windows rattled, the chicken cackled, the pig grunted, the cow mooed, and the horse whinnied, and the man got up, got dressed, and ran to the house of the wise woman.

"Wise Woman! Wise Woman!" cried the man. "Help me!"

"I think," said the wise woman, "that it is time to kick all those noisy animals out of your house."

Wearily, the man trudged home, and happily he put the horse, the cow, the pig, and the chicken back in the barn where they belonged. Then he lay down and fell asleep. The door creaked, but he did not wake up. The floorboards squeaked, but he did not wake up. The windows rattled, but he did not wake up. He slept soundly and peacefully until morning.

"At last," he sighed. "Peace and quiet!"

DIRECTIONS

Make the outline of a house at the lower left-hand corner of the flannel board (follow the directions in "Making Story Figures for the Flannel Board," pp. 5–6). Make the house big enough for the man's bed and all the animals to fit inside. The animals can overlap each other, and the chicken can perch on the bed.

Place the wise woman at the upper right of the flannel board; she can stay there for the entire story. The man alternately lies in his bed and stands in front of her.

Participation

Assign a child or group of children to each noise in the story: door, floorboards, windows, chicken, pig, cow, and horse. You can then conduct the group like a cacophonous sound-orchestra: gesture toward that particular child or group when it is time for them to provide their sound. You may wish to say, after the last noise that is mentioned: ". . . and all together they sounded like this." To keep things from getting out of hand, use a hand clap to let the group know when it is time to stop—and practice the art of stopping before you begin the story!

This story also makes a good short narrated play to present for parents or other children.

COW

CHICKEN

BED

PEACE AND QUIET

WISE WOMAN

MAN

188

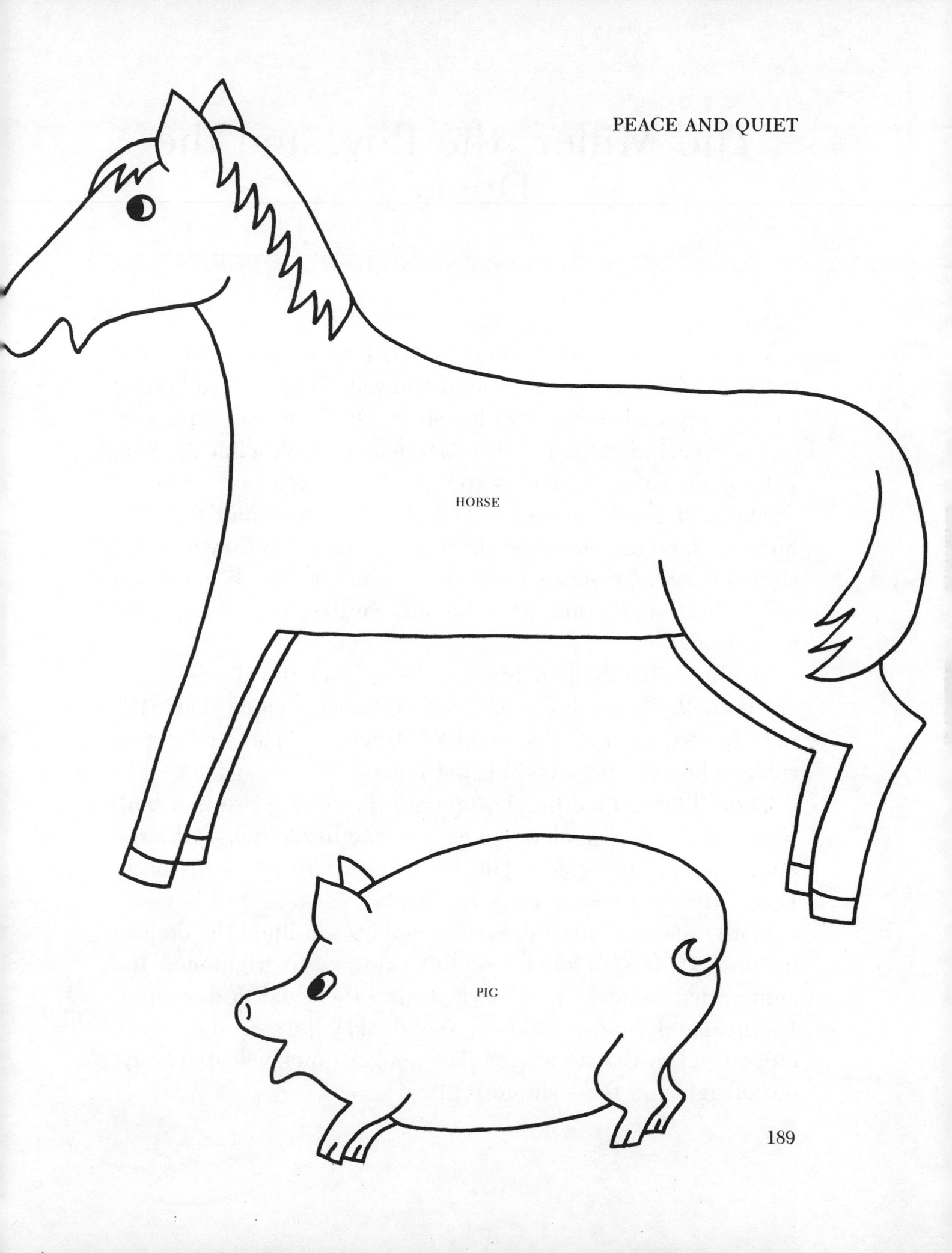

HORSE

PIG

189

The Miller, the Boy, and the Donkey

A FABLE BY AESOP

A MILLER and his son once set out to market with their donkey, which they were planning to sell. They walked behind the donkey and drove it with a stick. On their way, they met a man who chided them, "How is it that you have a fine donkey, yet you do not ride him? Is your donkey sick?"

The miller and his son looked at each other, and then the miller helped his son up on the donkey's back. As they traveled along, they met another stranger, who asked, "Is your son sick? Why does he ride, while his father walks? Where is respect for parents?"

So the miller helped his son down from the donkey, and got onto the beast himself. Another traveler came down the road toward them. "Aha!" said the traveler. "The strong man rides, while the poor child is left behind!"

The miller helped his son up onto the donkey, so that both were riding, when along came yet another critic. "Oh, the poor animal!" he cried. "You two brutes will break his back. Better that you should carry the donkey."

With great difficulty, the miller and his son lifted the donkey up onto their shoulders, but this position so frightened the animal that he kicked and kicked until they had to drop him. Unfortunately, they dropped the donkey just as they were crossing a bridge over a river. The donkey quickly floated away, out of sight, on the swift current.

"This should be a lesson to us," said the father. "We have tried to please all these people, and it has caused us to lose our donkey. Next time, we will do things our own way, and ignore advice that we have not asked for."

DIRECTIONS

The donkey is placed at the center of the flannel board, the man and the boy behind it to the right, as the story begins. The "critics" are placed to the left of the donkey, and are removed after they have spoken their piece. The donkey remains in one place as the man and boy try out different configurations of riding and walking. When the man and boy lift the donkey to their shoulders, place them a donkey-length apart and stand the donkey on their shoulders, removing the donkey when they have to drop him.

Follow-up

This story is a good one to act out, since children have such fun improvising lines for all the characters that criticize the miller and his son. The donkey can be a big stuffed duffel bag, a pillow, or a cardboard box.

MILLER

BOY

THE MILLER, THE BOY, AND THE DONKEY

DONKEY

THE MILLER, THE BOY, AND THE DONKEY

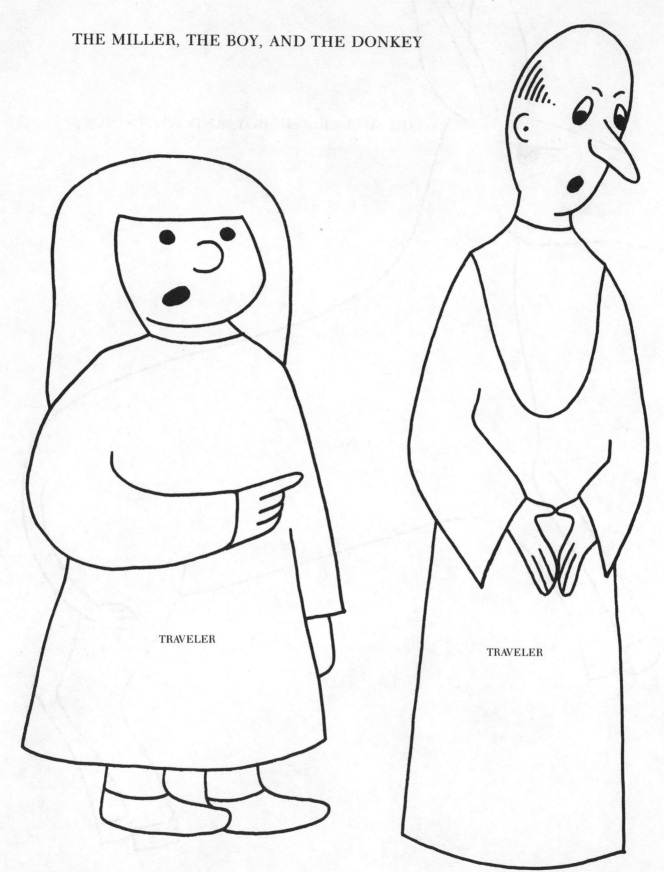

TRAVELER

TRAVELER

194

TRAVELER

TRAVELER

The Monkey and the Crocodile

AN INDIAN TALE

On an island in the middle of the river grew a tall mango tree. The fruits of the mango were fat. They were ripe. They sent their irresistible smell to the monkeys that lived by the riverbank.

One young monkey stood and stared sadly at the mango tree. He sniffed the air and whimpered.

"Ah, friend monkey!" A crocodile surfaced in the river. "I, too, have been wanting some of those delicious mangoes. Suppose we work together, as friends, to get them. I can swim across the river, but I cannot climb a tree. You can climb trees, but you cannot swim. So, jump on my back and I will carry you to the island. You can climb up the tree and eat all the mangoes you want, and throw the rest down to me."

The happy monkey leaped onto the crocodile's back and the crocodile swam away from the shore. But when they were no more than halfway to the island, the crocodile dived under the water. The poor monkey clung to the crocodile's scales and held his breath.

When the crocodile surfaced, the monkey gasped and coughed. "What are you doing, friend crocodile? You know I cannot breathe underwater."

"I am trying to drown you. Then, after I drown you, I will *eat* you."

"Oh dear," said the monkey. "That is so sad, so very sad. You are going to eat me, but you will not be able to taste my heart. It is the most delicious part of my body."

196

"I *will* eat your heart!" said the crocodile.

"No," said the monkey, "I don't think so. You see, I keep my heart in the mango tree. I left it there just last week when I was checking to see if the fruit was ripe."

"I will take you to the mango tree, and you will climb up and get your heart for me," hissed the crocodile. "Then I will eat you *and* your heart."

"Very well," replied the monkey, "since you insist."

The crocodile reached the far shore of the river and the monkey leaped onto the sand and scrambled up the tree. He began eating the ripe mangoes, and for good measure he threw some hard green ones down on the crocodile.

"Come down here!" growled the crocodile.

"Ha!" laughed the monkey. "A crocodile who believes that a monkey keeps his heart in a tree is as foolish as a monkey who calls a crocodile his friend."

The monkey spent many happy days on the island. But he knew he must find a way to get back across the river to his home. Around and around the island swam the crocodile, still very angry.

The monkey went down to the sandy shore where the river was very narrow. Soon enough, the crocodile appeared.

"I guess I might as well give up," said the monkey sadly. "I can't get back across the river, the mangoes are all gone, and I shall soon die of starvation."

The crocodile licked his crooked lips.

"So I might as well let you eat me," continued the monkey. "Open your mouth and I'll jump in."

The crocodile opened his mouth.

"Get just a little bit further back from the shore, so I can make a good final leap," called the monkey.

The crocodile backed up.

"Now open your mouth wide, wider, wider . . . so wide that you even have to close your eyes."

The crocodile opened his jaws as wide as they would go, and scrunched his eyes shut. Monkey made a stunning leap . . . *over* the crocodile's mouth, landing on his back, and with one more bound he was back on the bank of the river with his family and friends.

DIRECTIONS

Color the monkey and the crocodile on both sides. Cut the crocodile's mouth on the dotted line. When he opens his mouth at the end of the story, take the two parts of his mouth and separate them, making him open wide. Cut four or more mangoes and color them orange (or use orange felt). Place them on the tree, and place the tree to the left of the flannel board at the beginning of the story. When the monkey eats the mangoes, remove them from the board. The monkey begins the story standing on a small bit of sandy shore at the right of the flannel board.

Follow-up

This is an outstanding trickster tale, containing three delightful tricks. It can be the basis of a discussion of trust, lying, and trickery.

After the children know the story, two of them can perform it as a small play at the flannel board. One plays and moves the monkey, the other plays and moves the crocodile. It will need no narration—the children can stand at either side of the board and speak for their characters and move the story figures.

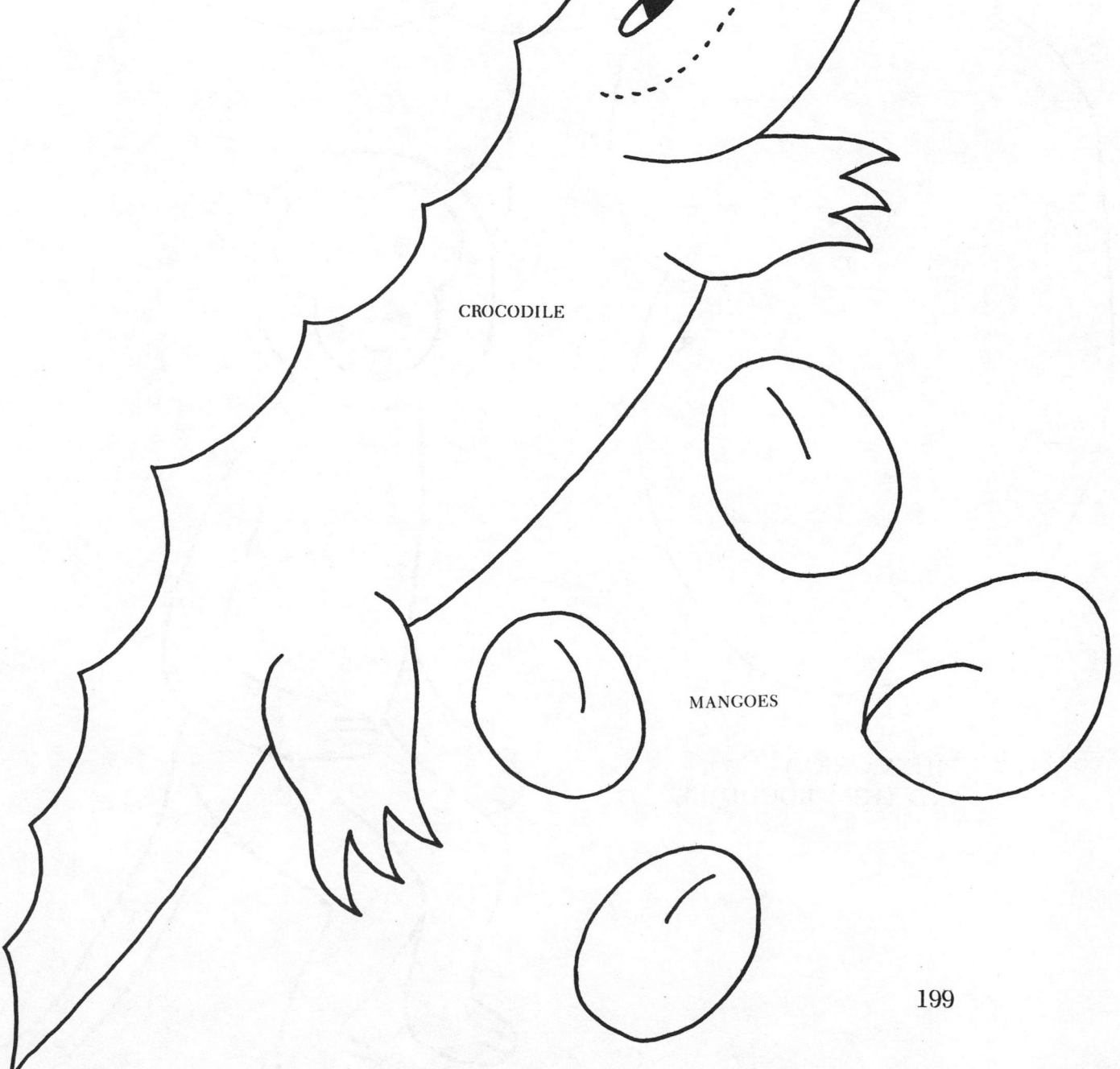

CROCODILE

MANGOES

199

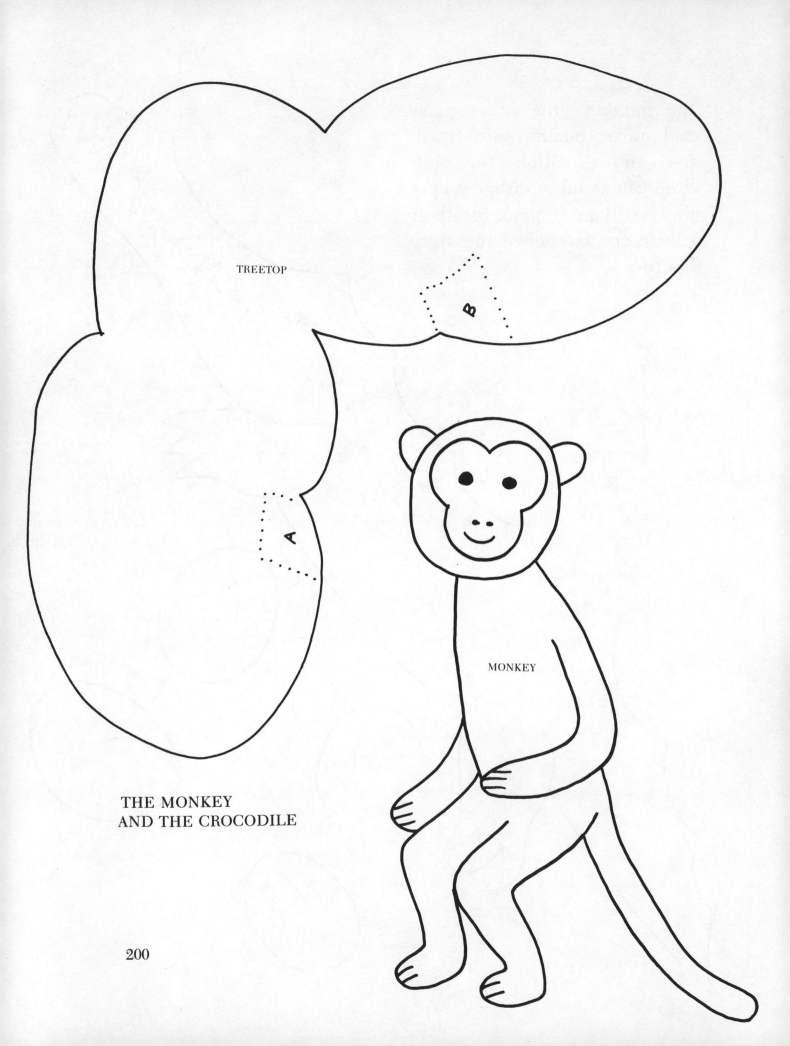

TREETOP

B

A

MONKEY

THE MONKEY
AND THE CROCODILE

200

201

SHORE

TREE TRUNK

ISLAND

A

B

THE MONKEY AND THE CROCODILE

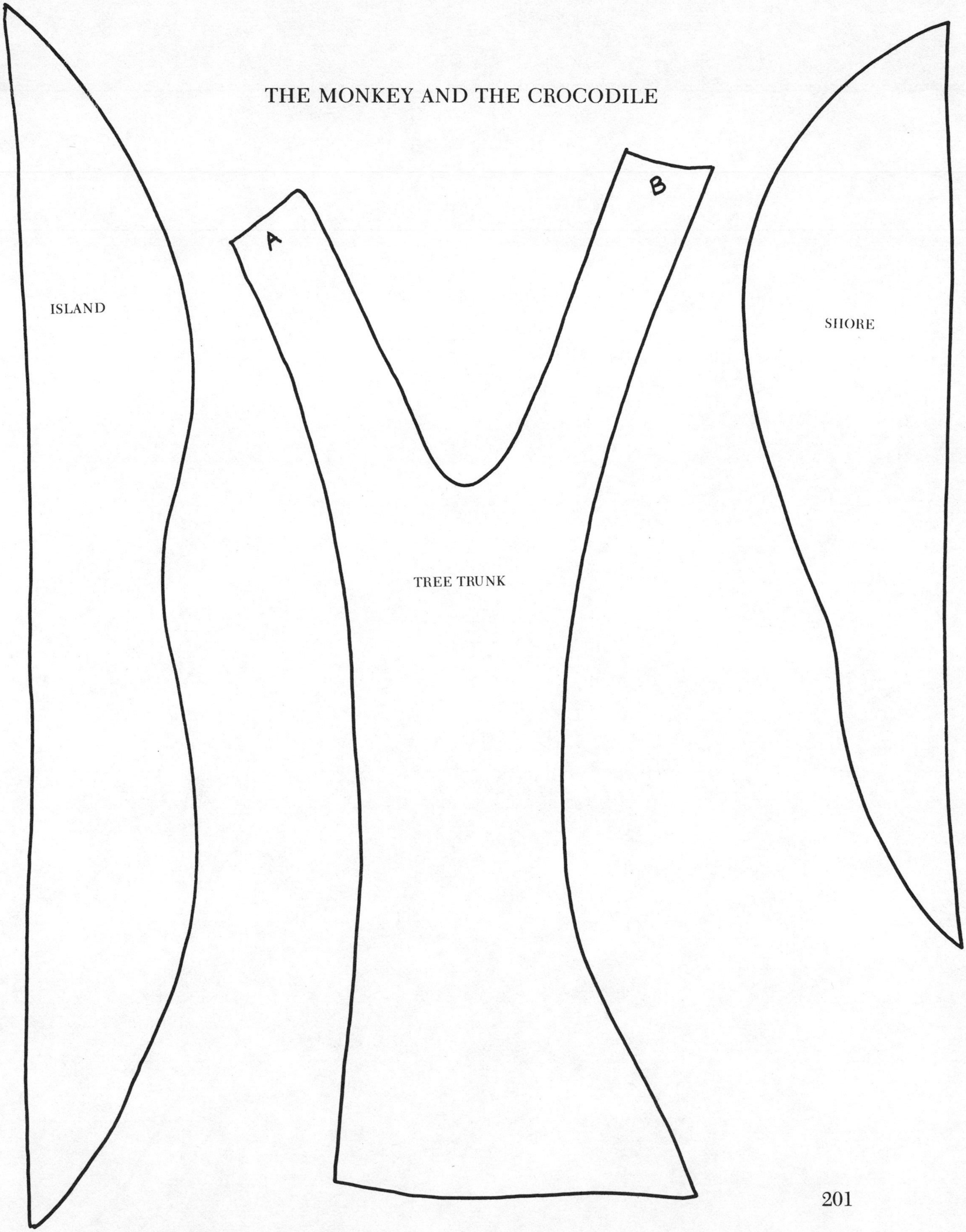

Bibliography

Flannel Boards

Bauer, Caroline Feller. *Handbook for Storytellers*. American Library Association, 1977.

Scott, Louise Binder, and J. J. Thompson. *Rhymes for Fingers and Flannelboards*. T. S. Denison, 1984.

Shoemaker, Kathryn E. *Creative Classroom*. Winston Press, 1980.

Storytelling

Baker, Augusta, and Ellin Greene. *Storytelling: Art and Technique*. R. R. Bowker, 1977.

Colwell, Eileen. *Storytelling*. Bodley Head, 1980.

Pellowski, Anne. *The World of Storytelling*. R. R. Bowker, 1977.

Schimmel, Nancy. *Just Enough to Make a Story*. Sisters' Choice Press, 1978.

Puppetry and Creative Dramatics

Gillies, Emily. *Creative Dramatics for All Children*. Association for Childhood Education International, 1973.

Heinig, Ruth Beall, and Lyda Stillwell. *Creative Dramatics for the Classroom Teacher*. Prentice-Hall, 1974.

Judy, Susan and Stephen. *Putting on a Play: A Guide to Writing and Producing Neighborhood Drama.* Scribner, 1982.

Sims, Judy. *Puppets for Dreaming and Scheming: A Puppet Source Book.* Early Stages, 1978.

Ward, Winifred. *Playmaking with Children from Kindergarten through Junior High School.* Second edition. Prentice-Hall, 1957.